To my dear friend

You are a such example
of a powerful, authentic,
woman leader.
I am blessed by your
friendship

On the Path to

Authentic Leadership

With so much love

Geraldine

xx

January 2018

Also by this author

Powerful Woman Tips: 100 Ways to Access and Live from Your Personal Power

Reclaim Your Power, Reclaim Your Life: Living Your Life as a Powerful Woman

Leading the Way in Diversity and Inclusion – Coaching Cards

Bringing Diversity and Inclusion to Life – Coaching Cards

Making Time BBC Publications – Part 3: The Juggle and the Struggle

with Mary Casey

From Diversity to Unity: Creating the Energy of Connection

with Catherine Brady

Are You Ready To Manage?

The Successful Manager

Getting To The Top

On the Path to

Authentic Leadership

The OPAL Way to Leadership Success

Geraldine M Bown

Acknowledgements

With thanks to the thousands of women I have worked with over the years who have shown me the meaning of resilience, patience, compassion and humour.

Special thanks to my closest female friends who have supported me, made me laugh and reminded me of my own power in those moments when I forgot.

Greatest thanks and appreciation to my daughters Lucy and Jessica who I am sure I neglected at times when I was working to help women! You have become amazing, powerful women in your own right. May you continue to inspire all the women you meet to find and live from their power, as you are doing. I love you both enormously.

Special mention and thanks to my daughter Jessica who has edited this and my other latest books and overseen the publication process for me.

Contents

Introduction

Many women are faced with wanting to develop a leadership style that best reflects their more natural feminine gender base while still being seen as credible.

In fact, this issue of leadership style and "fit" is one of the main reasons women choose to not put themselves forward, or if they do, find that their new role is difficult and stressful. The demands of leadership require the ability to demonstrate confidence, self-assurance, decisiveness, and a strong focus on results, of course.

As you move forward toward becoming a future leader, you need to have the ability to communicate a strong presence and be able to handle and initiate challenges with significant presentation and influencing abilities. It is critical that you learn to manage yourself and your messages so you project a strong presence while maintaining your authentic feminine base.

This book addresses key concerns of women in corporate organisations and will help you to prepare for that important leadership role.

You will benefit from this book if:

- You have recently been promoted into a leadership position
- You are keen to progress into a leadership position
- You are reluctant to adopt a masculine style and want to develop your own unique leadership voice
- You want to increase your self-confidence to match your competence and contribute fully to organisational success
- You are preparing for leadership and need to be able to develop your own personal power so you can become an inspirational leader

The OPAL way to leadership success can help you to raise your profile at work, raise your confidence levels, and help you to access and work from your authentic power base.

Here's how the OPAL way will help you. You'll be able to:

☑ **Assess your own power base and discover the basis for your own personal authentic power**

(So you will know exactly which situations lead you to feel powerful and powerless; understand where your authentic power lies and realise the benefits of accessing your own personal power.)

☑ **Remove the obstacles on your path to authentic leadership by overcoming the internal barriers in your head**

(And switch your mindset from a negative one to a positive one giving you benefits in all areas of your life – not just your career.)

☑ **Synthesise the masculine/feminine energies in yourself and identify when you need to use each**

(Yes, I do believe that there are major differences between most men and most women in style and context so let's move the discussion away from "better" and "worse" and look at valuing all of them and providing people with easy access to each.)

☑ **Develop a leadership presence so you are seen as a leader even before you get your leadership position**

(Let's examine exactly what "presence" looks like, because it's not easy to define.)

☑ **Reduce your stress levels**

(By examining the effectiveness of your short-term solutions to stress and laying down a strategy for dealing with stress long term.)

☑ **Discover the essential qualities of an authentic leader and draw up a plan for acquiring then**

(Including exploring the connection between authenticity, inspiration and leadership.)

☑ **Identify your biggest challenges in managing home/work integration more effectively and draw up an action plan for overcoming them**

(Hint: what you believe about your responsibilities as a wife/partner and as a mother will be critical here – as will the ability to say 'no'.)

☑ **Examine your communication style and sharpen up its effectiveness so that your message is never mistaken**

(And that means making sure your verbal and non-verbal messages are saying the same thing as well as being able to handle formal presentations.)

The book is divided into three parts: Exploring Concepts, Overcoming Obstacles and Taking Action. In the first part we'll look at ideas and insights to help you to think about your own leadership style. Part two will look at what might need to change in your thinking, and in your life, so that there is nothing that will hinder your progress into leadership. The final part, Taking Action, is where you'll be encouraged to be pro-active about your leadership presence and journey.

Each part has three chapters and within these are a series of self-reflection questions about the issues raised in that chapter. I recommend getting a notebook to jot down your insights and reflections and to complete the questions. This can then become a developmental plan as you work through this book. The questions are there to help you to reflect on the issues that are pertinent to you right now. You don't necessarily have to answer them all, but thinking through these issues may highlight something for you that is worth further exploration.

Part 1
Exploring Concepts

Chapter 1

Concepts of Power

If you are a leader you will have power. The question is, what kind of power and how will you use it? How comfortable are you with being in a position of power? Do you recognise the power within yourself whether you have a position of power or not? And is power different for men and women?

In this chapter:

- ▸ Four external sources of power
- ▸ Our comfort levels around power sources
- ▸ Your internal source of power
- ▸ The attributes and benefits when you operate from your authentic, powerful self

Four external sources of power

Before we go any further we're going to start straight away with our first self-reflection exercise.

Self-Reflection 1

Think about what *you* mean by power. How would you complete
the sentence 'Power is...'?
Note down your answer and hold your definition in mind as we look
a little deeper at where we get our power.

We're going to look at four external sources of power:

- Position power
- Connection power
- Expert power
- Personality power

Position Power

This is the power bestowed on you by virtue of your job or role. As soon as you move into a management position you have a certain amount of power over the people who report to you. People on the board of directors of a company have power over the senior management team. If you are the chairperson of a committee you are given power to conduct and control meetings – this kind of power comes with the territory of the job.

Connection Power

This is the power you have by virtue of your connection to someone with power. Michelle Obama had a lot of connection power when she was First Lady because she had the ear of the President. A personal assistant to a CEO has a lot of connection power and in this case connection power can translate as gatekeeper power – you can't get to the CEO without getting past the PA. Or you might have connection power because of an existing relationship, e.g. someone you used to work closely with in another company now works in your company.

Expert Power

You can have expert power no matter what level you are at an organisation. You might be the computer games geek who people come to for advice; you might be the eBay expert and run little groups for people at lunchtime about how to get the best out of eBay; you might be a cooking expert or a fly fishing expert. People, even those with more position power than you, defer to *you* in a particular area because of the expert knowledge you have.

Personality Power

This is the power that some people have by virtue of their personal charisma and dynamism. These people can get people to follow them and do what they want because they inspire trust in people; people love them and love hearing what they have to say. The down side of personality power is that bullies also have this kind of power. They use the force of their personalities to beat people down and people fear them and so do what they want. This, of course, is an abuse of power.

So what sources of power do you have? This is a good place to pause and make some notes in your notebook.

Self-Reflection 2

Write down on a scale of 1-10 how much power you have in each of the four areas mentioned, where 1 is no power at all and 10 is complete power. Look at the areas where you have little or no power.
Do you want to change that? How can you change it?

Your comfort levels around power sources

Now we're going to look at how comfortable you are around power, when you feel powerful and when you feel powerless.

Self-Reflection 3

Write down some of the times you feel powerful and some of the times when you feel powerless. Do this before reading on.

Here are some of the times when women have said they feel powerless:

- *When I have no control.*
- *When I don't have the right skills.*
- *When I've made a mistake.*
- *When I'm criticised.*
- *When I can't meet another's needs.*
- *When I feel I'm being excluded.*

What about when women feel powerful? They said they feel powerful when:

- *I receive praise or positive feedback.*
- *I get what I want.*
- *I say 'no'.*
- *I do a good job.*
- *People ask me for advice.*
- *I empower others.*

Have you had similar ones? There are times for us all when we feel powerful and when we feel powerless and of course the ideal is that we can access our personal power even in those situations that are capable of draining our power. But before we look at the fifth area of power – our personal power – it's important to distinguish between our comfort levels around power.

It's probably easy to think of the times when we are powerful and comfortable. These might be when we are leading a group, making a decision or receiving praise from our team.

But what about some of the times when we are powerful but uncomfortable? How about soon after a promotion? Or when you have to make a difficult decision? Or when you have to criticise the poor performance of someone?

Sometimes, even if we are powerless, we might be comfortable in some situations. Such as:

- Being a team member not a leader, and not having to carry the responsibility
- When you don't have to make a difficult decision, someone else has to
- When you can't be held responsible for what happens

And finally there will be times when we are powerless and uncomfortable, for example watching the news, or when there is nothing you can do to ease someone's pain, or carrying out a decision you don't agree with.

The important thing to remember about power is that there are some advantages to being powerless, but the more you move up your career ladder, the more you will be assuming a role and a job which will require you to step up and step into your power.

Self-Reflection 4

I want you to think carefully about this issue of comfort and discomfort around power. Look at your external sources of power from Self-Reflection 2 and try to identify if there is a link between those sources and your comfort levels.
For instance, if you know you have connection power; how comfortable are you using it? If you know you have position power; how comfortable do you feel when you have to pull rank?

If you feel uncomfortable with power it can hold you back as much as your feelings about feeling powerless.

All of the four external sources of power depend on someone being a "more than" to someone else's "less than". It depends on power *over* someone else. Many women are uncomfortable with this approach. We know what it's like to be treated as a "less than" and we don't want to be "more thans" if we perceive that in so doing we have to treat people as "less thans".

Your internal source of power

There is another kind of power, however, that we can get in touch with and that is our authentic power; our inner power – our personal power. Your comfort levels around power will depend very much on how much of your personal power – your authentic power – you can access.

First of all let me be clear about what I mean by personal power. Personal power is about *presence*. It's connected with what uplifts, dignifies and ennobles. Power that equates with force tries to move something from A to B whereas authentic power is still and complete – it needs nothing from the outside to feed it. It is a state of being. And although force can bring satisfaction in the short term, personal power brings joy and meaning to our lives. So by personal power I don't mean power that you are given from an external source but rather presence and authenticity, which comes from within.

The bad news is that when women saw power only in terms of masculine and feminine power, many women embraced a masculine version of power concerned with control and command in order to succeed. And, to be fair, many would not have succeeded if they hadn't done that. But that kind of power doesn't necessarily sit well with us. This way of being is not who we feel we are at our core. Look at what Nancy Kline says about this in her book *Women and Power*.

Men and women live in different cultures. Women are taught, from their earliest years, that their excellence as women will be judged by how they interact with people and by whether or not people will flourish in their care. Men are taught that their excellence as men will be judged by the way that they control people, by how well they promote themselves, and by whether or not they stay 'on top'. These two cultures create very different kinds of leaders. Controlling leaders keep people from thinking; their purpose is to herd others. Interactive leaders ignite people's thinking; their purpose is to launch others.

There is an opportunity for women to tune into the leadership skills they already possess and be instrumental in helping the organisations they work for move forward, become more effective, and be more rewarding places to be in and to work in. In order to do this, women need to be trained to trust their own thinking, to value their culture as women, and to change the corridors of power as they walk them.

To change the corridors of power as they walk them – what a lovely phrase! Now of course things are changing. Not all men are command and control freaks and not all women are nurturing. I spoke with a woman recently from Eastern Europe who was brought up in a socialist regime where equality was paramount and there were no differences between her and her male friends and colleagues. She felt she wasn't disadvantaged in any way by her gender conditioning. She is now working in a global firm where the company culture could be defined as masculine. And, although she is perfectly at home there, she is perceived to have a masculine style and gets feedback that she appears to be lacking in empathy, which people expect of her because she is a woman!

We don't want to become masculine in order to succeed; we want to be true to our feminine base *and* we want to be credible *and* we might have to do all this within a masculine culture. So, how can we do that?

The answer is to connect with our deep, authentic selves and operate from a personal power base that will not only be sustaining for us but bring rich rewards for our organisations too.

The good news is that we – and I mean women – have a deep well of authenticity and presence within us. I believe that we have wisdom within us handed down from generations and ages of wise women. Women's authentic strength is magnificent and this book is going to help you to access yours and bring it to the fore in your job, and in your life.

Many women are now shunning the masculine model and wanting to be different kinds of leaders but are finding it difficult to find their authentic voice in the current climates in their organisations. One company did some research with their most senior female engineers to find out at first hand what was going on for them. They wanted to look at what barriers they felt were holding them back. Let's look at what they said. And then we'll see if any of them apply to you.

The first issue was that of **low confidence.** They felt that they didn't have a voice, it was difficult to challenge the status quo and they just didn't seem to fit in or were even excluded. And, even if you do have a voice, if you have to shout just to get attention so you can make your point, many women decide it's just not worth the effort.

The second issue was that of **low entitlement.** By this I mean not being comfortable claiming your place as an equal, being tentative and not expecting the same rewards. I speak to people these days that assume the pay battle has been won – that men and women get equal pay for equal value when in fact they don't. There are still huge gaps between men and women and women are less likely to "go for it" than men are. Women are more inclined to adopt the attitude of 'I'll see what the organisation has in mind for me' as opposed to assessing their own worth and putting themselves forward.

The third issue was about **owning accomplishments** – how they felt about what they had accomplished. Many women play down their achievements whereas many men talk theirs up. Women often stay in the background, and don't want to bring attention to their good work. They also hold back, especially if they feel their approach isn't valued. And they are more likely to see their accomplishments as "less than" when compared to men's accomplishments.

Self-Reflection 5

Which of the following elements of low confidence, sense of low entitlement and owning accomplishments apply to you?

- *I don't feel I have a voice.*
- *I don't challenge the status quo.*
- *I just don't seem to fit in.*
- *I feel I am excluded.*
- *I don't feel comfortable claiming my place as an equal.*
- *I'm tentative in my approach.*
- *I don't expect equal rewards.*
- *I 'wait and see' when it comes to promotion.*
- *I don't put myself forward for opportunities.*

Choose two out of this list to work on from today.

We have to get to a place where we can design a new power platform for ourselves no matter what our position, our connections, our expertise or our personalities. And we have to remove the blocks to the feminine and authentic wisdom already inside us so we can release it into the world.

The attributes and benefits when you operate from your authentic, powerful self

L et's look at 10 attributes of those who have personal power so we can see how we measure up and what we might need to do.

Powerful women...

- Have high self-esteem
- Have energy
- Take personal responsibility
- Deal with their guilt issues
- Don't worry about things they can't control
- See the gift in every situation
- Get their own needs fulfilled
- Make things happen
- Help others get what they want
- Energise people around them

Let's examine these attributes.

Powerful woman have high self-esteem

Self-esteem is different to confidence. We can learn how to act confidently even if we have low self-esteem, and we might need to do this while we build up our self-esteem. But self-esteem is related to how we feel about ourselves – how we value our own worth – and there seems to be a direct correlation between high self-esteem and great performance. High self-esteem is critical for excellent individual performance as well as team performance.

Powerful women have energy

People who are in touch with their personal power have unlimited energy. Most women I know have tons of energy, and they need to have to get through the demands of a job, organising a home, dealing with extended family issues not to mention trying to fit in exercise, seeing friends and doing good deeds... But with no access to their personal power all these activities deplete their energy and drain them of internal resources.

Women who are coming from a powerful authentic base know when to say no, know how to take care of themselves and know how to deal with their guilt and worry issues. You need to have high energy to be able to set priorities, make choices and take responsibility for those choices and your life.

Powerful women take personal responsibility

An authentic woman knows that she has to take responsibility for how her life is unfolding. Blame and authenticity cannot live together. No one can make us feel anything without our permission. The principle to remember is: *Choose – and choose again*. We make a choice and then we implement it and live with it. Then we get some new information. It may be 10 minutes later, 10 days or 10 months and we want to make a different choice. That's fine. It doesn't mean we made a bad decision or a wrong choice in the first place; it means we made the best choice and decision based on the information we had at the time. Now we need to choose again, always realising that it *is* a choice.

Personal responsibility means that we make a choice and are prepared to live with the consequences until we want to make another choice. I hear women say: 'I hate my job but I can't leave it; I have bills to pay and children to take care of so I have no choice but to stay in my job.' Well, actually, you are choosing to stay in your job because paying the bills is more important to you than being happy at work. So accept that you *are* making a choice and do whatever you can at work to make it happier for you *until* you decide that your health is maybe suffering and you'll take a lower paid job and manage the money somehow so you can be healthier and happier.

Powerful women deal with their guilt issues

Powerful women know how to deal with guilt. Guilt is a useless emotion and drains our personal power in the flash of a thought.

We cannot live in the world of "should" and "ought" and "supposed to". Those words signify that we really don't want to but if we don't we'll feel really guilty. So next time you feel a "should" coming on ask yourself: what will be the consequence if I don't do this, and can I live with that? If you decide that you wouldn't be able to live with the consequences then go ahead and do whatever it is – but now you are doing it from a place of want, not ought, so you can do it with graciousness. And if you choose not to do it you are already prepared to face the consequences for you have chosen them. Now your courage will see you through. We're going to come back to guilt in a later chapter.

The powerful woman develops courage, practises graciousness and leaves guilt outside the door where it belongs.

Powerful women don't worry about things they can't control

We have to be clear about what is in our control and what isn't. When our children go to school, or the first time they go on holiday with their friends, or when they leave home to go to university, we are not going to be by their sides. We have to trust that our parenting and their own common sense will see them through tough times and of course we will be there when they need help. But we can't live their lives for them – they have their own journeys to take and their own lessons to learn.

Worry is a useless emotion. If you can do something about something then do it. If you can't then you just have to trust that things are unfolding exactly as they are meant to. You need your energy for the things you *can* control that you need to take action on.

Powerful women see the gift in every situation

This is an interesting one. This is based on the premise that everything that happens, happens *for* us and not *to* us. And we need to see everything that happens as information. What is this telling me? What do I need to know here? How could this be for my good? What is the gift here? We all know of situations when something happens which seemed terrible at the time, like losing our job – then two years later hear ourselves saying, 'I felt so bad at the time but it was the best thing that could have happened because as a result I decided to have a career change and now I have this wonderful position doing something I love.'

The skill we have to acquire is being able to see the gift in the situation to help us *through* the situation. Sometimes bad things happen and we have to step up to a higher level in order to cope and trust that everything is really OK, no matter how it looks now or how much pain we are in. We will then access a calm inner state of being, which is where our personal power and authenticity lie.

Powerful women get their own needs fulfilled

This is the thing that busy women find so hard to do in my experience. We spend so long running around making sure everyone else is OK that we put ourselves to the bottom of the list and only take the amount for ourselves that can be squeezed at the end. Powerful people don't do this. In order to be operating at your best all the time you have to make sure that you are at an optimum level – emotionally, physically, mentally and spiritually. If you don't address *your* needs, bit-by-bit everything else will start to fall apart around you. It's like they say on aeroplanes: put your own breathing mask on before helping anyone else with theirs. We have to give ourselves time first to identify what our needs are and then to look at what we need to do to get them fulfilled. *Then* we are in the best place to support others.

All these points are related to the attributes and benefits to us personally if we access our personal power. They are also pre-requisites. Unless we can take care of our own needs, stop worrying, deal with our guilt issues, take personal responsibility and see the gift in every situation we will never have high energy or increase our self-esteem. None of these things are to do with what position we hold, or how much we know; they are about who we are and how we are operating in every area of our lives. They are about how personally powerful we are.

Self-Reflection 6

Write down which of these attributes you think you need to work on next.
What are two things you can do for each that will help you get there?

Once we have access to these things here's what happens.

Powerful women make things happen, help others get what they want and energise those around them

We make things happen, we help others to get what *they* want and we energise people around us. Our personal power doesn't only help us to get what we want and live a productive life: it rubs off on those around us so we can help them do the same.

Our personal power is the door through which everything else comes.

Self-Reflection 7

Write your new definition of power. One that will be a working definition
for you as you go forward.

I want to end this chapter with a thought from Marianne Williamson about power
and presence.

> *Our deepest fear is not that we are inadequate. Our deepest fear is that we are
> powerful beyond measure. It is our light, not our darkness that most frightens
> us. We ask ourselves, who am I to be brilliant, gorgeous, talented, fabulous?
> Actually, who are you not to be? You are a child of God. Your playing small
> does not serve the world. There is nothing enlightened about shrinking so
> that other people won't feel insecure around you. We are all meant to shine,
> as children do. We were born to make manifest the glory of God that is within
> us. It is not just in some of us; it is in everyone. And as we let our own light
> shine, we unconsciously give other people permission to do the same. As we
> are liberated from our own fear, our presence automatically liberates others.*

You are *already* powerful – you just need to uncover the blocks to the personal
power that is already within you. We'll cover this in Part 2: Overcoming Obstacles.

Chapter 2

Concepts of Masculine/Feminine Differences

There are still relatively few women leaders. Do the fundamental differences between men and women play a part here? Do you need masculine qualities to be a leader? And do feminine qualities have a place in leadership roles?

In this chapter:

- ▸ The difference between male and masculine and female and feminine
- ▸ Brain and socialisation differences between men and women
- ▸ Masculine/feminine differences regarding power, communication and relationships
- ▸ Perceptions of differences
- ▸ Harmonising the masculine and feminine

The difference between male and masculine and female and feminine

The first point I want to address is the contentious aspect of talking about male and female differences. You'll notice this chapter is entitled *masculine and feminine* differences, and it's important to clear up the connection between male and masculine and female and feminine.

There does seem to be an accepted scale of masculine and feminine styles which we will be discussing, and while it is probably true that many men would be nearer the masculine end of the scale, and many women would be nearer the feminine end of the scale, this isn't true for all men and all women. We all know women who exhibit what are thought of as masculine characteristics (competitiveness, directness, independence) and we all know men who are much more in touch with what would be called their feminine side (nurturing, supportive, connecting).

So from the outset, there are three very important points I want to make:

1. Leaders need a blend of masculine and feminine characteristics.

They need to be comfortable with all points on the masculine/feminine scale, and they need to be able to draw on all of those characteristics as the situation demands. Whether or not you are single or married in the conventional sense, I would say that the real marriage we all need to engage in is the marriage of the masculine and feminine inside ourselves.

2. Neither of these styles is necessarily better than the other.

The problem is that the masculine style has predominated in organisations so people most comfortable operating from this masculine platform, who have been mainly men, are the ones who have been promoted. This is why many women have learned to adopt a masculine style even when it's not their preferred style, so they will be valued in the masculine culture they are working in. And the people who work in the departments where soft skills (as they are so-called) are required – like HR – won't be valued as much as those who work in the operations or sales functions.

3. Perception is key.

If women are presumed to be operating from a feminine platform, and that platform is devalued, then it follows that women will be devalued. They will be perceived as "less thans". Women are still being treated as "less thans" in organisations, communities and society at large, in a million different ways. But the perception knife can cut men too. They might be expected to behave in a certain masculine way where status and hierarchy is important, and therefore find it very difficult to ask for and accept help, so they could be isolated and very stressed.

Some women say that they will act masculine and wait until they are in a position of power and *then* they will incorporate more of their feminine characteristics but it's hard to swim with the sharks without becoming one. And if you are really a dolphin, why would you want to swim with the sharks anyway? There are many women now who won't compromise on their own personal values and adopt an alien way of being in order to progress. But the truth is that many organisations *do* operate from a masculine style, so how on earth can women progress in these organisations and remain authentic to their core values? We looked a little at this in Chapter 1 when we looked at power.

Now we're going to go into more detail about these two styles and have a close look at some masculine/feminine differences and some male/female differences. Your job will be to look at yourself, your male and female colleagues and your organisations very closely in order to decide for yourself which characteristics you have, which you want to change, and which you want to develop.

Brain and socialisation differences between men and women

Let's start by looking at whether there are actually any brain differences between men and women. We know our bodies are different – but are our brains? It seems the experts are divided about this.

Michael Gurian, social philosopher and author of *What Could He Be Thinking?* has claimed to identify approximately 100 structural differences between male and female brains.

He writes:

> *Men, because we tend to compartmentalise our communication into a smaller part of the brain, tend to be better at getting right to the issue. The more female brain will gather a lot of material, gather a lot of information, feel a lot, hear a lot, sense a lot.*

While in *The Essential Difference*, Simon Baron-Cohen writes that the female brain is predominantly hard-wired for empathy and that the male brain is predominantly hard-wired for understanding and building systems.

He compares empathising and systemising:

> Empathising *is the drive to identify another person's emotions and thoughts and to respond to these with an appropriate emotion. The empathiser intuitively figures out how people are feeling and how to treat people with care and sensitivity. This is the female brain's way.*
>
> Systemising *is the drive to analyse and explore a system, to extract underlying rules that govern the behaviour of a system and the drive to construct systems. This belongs in the domain of the male brain.*

And Louan Brizendine writes in *The Female Brain*:

> *Women have an eight-lane superhighway for processing.*

And:

> *The main hub for emotion and memory formation is larger in a woman's brain.*

In summary, these facts and theories about biological differences, brains and hormones, seem to show that women:

- Gather a lot of material / information
- Feel a lot, hear a lot, sense a lot
- Are hard-wired for empathy
- Have the drive to identify another person's emotions and thoughts
- Care about how others feel and about treating people with care and sensitivity
- Are very good at processing emotion
- Have a larger hub for emotion and memory formation
- Are more flexible and find it easier to multi-task

So the characteristics that would result are:

- Empathy
- Care
- Sensitivity
- Ability to verbalise feelings
- Better verbal skills
- Multi-tasking
- Flexibility

That's what some people are saying who believe that men and women do indeed have different brain structures. I wonder if these are true for you? For myself, I would say that I am actually good at getting to the heart of the issue. And bringing clarity to a complex situation is a strength of mine. I would also say that I am more inclined to want to analyse and explore a system or situation so I can understand what's going on, rather than just empathise.

My roommate at college many years ago was a very empathetic person and mutual friends used to say: 'We come to Dee if we want sympathy and we come to you if we want to know what to do!' I wasn't sure that I was terribly thrilled with that assessment to be honest. Yet these traits, which were evident in me many years ago, are described by Gurian and Baron-Cohen as coming from a male brain. So, if they are right, then as a female I wasn't born with these masculine characteristics,

I must have developed them as I was growing up.

In her book *Delusions of Gender*, Cordelia Fine, a researcher at Melbourne University, argues that while there may be slight variations in the brains of women and men, the wiring is soft, not hard: *'It is flexible, malleable and changeable.'*

Lise Eliot, an associate professor based at the Chicago Medical School would agree. She says, *'There is almost nothing we do with our brains that is hard-wired. Every skill, attribute and personality trait is molded by experience.'*

While people may argue about genetics and the brain, nearly everyone agrees that the socialisation process is key in shaping our abilities, skills and behaviour.

Our gender blueprinting begins the minute we are born. We are bombarded with messages about life: the *good* things and the *bad* things, the *right* way and the *wrong* way.

Socialisation differences include:

Upbringing — Different traits, roles, behaviours, attitudes and aptitudes that males and females are expected to display towards work, family, appearance, fun and entertainment, dos and don'ts.

Culture — The social construction of differences between the sexes pertaining to a particular culture.

For example:

Girls	Boys
Avoid competition/confrontation in order not to lose femininity and friends	More competitive and assertive self-reliant and independent
Respectful, polite, friendly, humble	More chance for problem solving and conflict resolution
If you work hard you will get ahead	Work hard but also take risks
Forge friendships	Gain visibility
Success as a team member	Get the credit for their own success

And of course there are cultural differences and national characteristics to take into account. I am British and the prevalent attitude of having a stiff upper lip – putting up with things, not being loud and brash – applies to men as well as women.

I wonder what cultural and national characteristics are evident in you?

Self-Reflection 1

What messages were you given as a girl growing up? Do you think any of these messages have hindered your progress in the workplace?

However you have been shaped, whether by your brain or your socialisation process, we now need to look at differences between men and women as they get played out in work, and in life, too.

So with the big assumption that most masculine qualities are evident in most men, and most feminine qualities are evident in most women, let's consider what that looks like in the workplace for men and women working together.

Masculine/feminine differences regarding power, communication and relationships

We're going to look at some male/female differences in relation to three areas: basis of power; communication, and relationships. And as we look at each area we need to consider whether these differences are generalisations, stereotypes or useful distinctions. As ever, you need to assess what is true for you and what that means for you in terms of how you want to behave and how you want to be seen at work.

The overriding principle is that men tend to see themselves – certainly in relation to other men – as separate and different while women see themselves as close and the same. This is very closely tied to where we think our basis of power is. Look at the table below.

Area 1 – Basis of Power

Masculine qualities	Feminine qualities
Independence/hierarchy/status	Intimacy and connections
Self-focused	Supportive and other focused
Competitive	Co-operative
Confronting	Consulting
Directing	Nurturing
Seeks status and respect	Seeks connection, rapport and closeness
Networking used more for power	Networking used more for relationships
Independence is power	Independence is alienation
Dependence is weakness	Interdependence is strength
Life is a contest for individuals to win	The community is the source of power

The first quality is really the key one: men function based on a hierarchical model. Status is very important to them and competitiveness is needed to ensure that you can rise in the hierarchy. They see life as a contest in which they are continually tested and must perform well to avoid the risk of failure.

For women, intimacy and connections are far more important and they see their community as their basis of power. They would rather maintain a friendship than engage in a personal conflict and are more likely to be supportive and focused on the other, or others, rather than on themselves. For men, independence is power. Whereas for women, independence implies alienation. So the masculine qualities of competitiveness, confrontation and direction are counter to the more feminine qualities of co-operation, consultation, and nurturing.

Now of course, none of these qualities are good or bad per se. There will be times when clear direction is needed, without consultation. And most organisations are competing with other organisations in the market place. Yet it is also true that they are now more inclined to want to partner with their suppliers rather than dictate to them.

Even attitudes to networking are different. Think also about your male and female colleagues. What do you notice? Who are the most successful people in your organisation? Are the most successful women operating from a masculine angle regarding these qualities relating to power? What gets rewarded where you work?

Self-Reflection 2

Have you observed or experienced any male/female differences in the area of attitudes to power? Note them.

Area 2 – Communication

Masculine qualities	Feminine qualities
Prefer to talk	Prefer to listen
Talk to report and negotiate status — who is up and who is down	Talk for rapport and tend to focus on connection
Like to give advice	Seek to be understood and understand
Control emotions	Express emotions
Make statements	Ask questions
Listening is a submissive activity	Listening to empathise builds trust
Holding centre stage — 'I'	Being one of the group — 'We'
Speak and hear a language of status	Use rituals to establish equality
Direct and pointed language	Indirect, tentative language
Comfortable displaying superiority	Fear that displaying superiority will bring about alienation

Male and female differences in communication have been written about extensively. I love Deborah Tannen's books *You Just Don't Understand* and *Talking From 9 to 5*. If you are interested in further reading on these topics then I would recommend both these books.

You can see the list of qualities for yourself. There are a few things I want to mention which frame all of these qualities. One is to do with the reason we have for talking in the first place! Deborah Tannen believes that many men talk to negotiate status and establish who is "up" and who is "down", whereas many women are more focused on connection. Women are often seeking the gift of understanding whereas men often give the gift of advice. And we can see a similar thing in relation to listening. For some men, the act of listening frames one as lower. But when women listen they are attempting to reinforce connections and establish rapport and they expect it to be reciprocal. But if men are viewing listening through the lens of status, then women are casting themselves in a subordinate position and men will see them that way.

Similarly, asking for information sets yourself as subordinate to the person or expert you are asking who knows the answer – even if that person is a stranger. I'm sure I'm not the only woman who has been lost in a car with a man who refuses to stop and ask someone for directions, preferring to try a variety of routes and if necessary be late, rather than admit he needs to ask someone for help.

Giving feedback is an interesting area. Many men feel that women don't tell them directly enough if they are doing something wrong. Some women feel uncomfortable giving negative feedback because they don't want the other to feel bad (because they know that *they* would feel bad if they got negative feedback). On the other hand, some women feel that they don't get the feedback they need to improve (because their male managers fear they will be upset) and that men don't tell them directly enough when they do well.

As we can see, this area of communication is fraught with the potential for assumptions and misunderstandings.

Finally, I want to mention the use of rituals. Why do women apologise so much and put themselves down and shrug off compliments? Sometimes, when women say I'm sorry, it's not really an apology but rather a statement that: 'I'm sorry it happened'. Tannen also points out that women often want to establish equality. (I like your hair. Oh I don't think he did it right, but I love *your* cut.) Women use these rituals to put themselves down and depend on the other person to round off the ritual and pull them back up. But in a conversation with a man who operates from a status platform, he will be happy to maintain his status, and not pull her back up. So he will reinforce his one-up position and she will accept it.

Here are some quotes from Deborah Tannen's book *Talking From 9 to 5*.

> It is not only useful but also necessary to understand the cultural patterns that influence our ways of speaking. Not talking about them doesn't make the stereotypes go away. It just gives them free rein to affect our lives and robs us of the understanding necessary to change them.
>
> All styles are equally valid as styles and they can all work well in some situations with others who share that style. But that does not mean that all styles work equally well in every situation. And that is why, in the end, the best

style is one that is flexible.

If men and women talk differently, it is not because they can't talk any other way but because they don't want to. Our ways of talking reflect the ways we assume a good person talks and we get our sense of how we should be a good person by observing the others we talk to with whom we identify.

What is your preferred communication style? And what have you noticed about your female and male colleagues? Maybe already, you are seeing some qualities that you want to be less strong and some that you want to strengthen. In some situations women need to be comfortable holding centre stage, and speaking up (as we will see in Chapter 7) and maybe in some situations we need to control our emotions more. But if we already have some skills in the areas of listening and establishing connections then we don't want to let go of these qualities.

Self-Reflection 3

Have you observed or experienced any male/female differences in the area of communication? Note them.

Area 3 – Relationships

Much has been written about male/female relationships and there is no need to repeat all that here. We mentioned earlier in this chapter some of the gender differences between girls and boys growing up. What is of particular note, though, is the impact that team sports has had in boys' and girls' education. Some of the most insightful research pertaining to gender issues and differences in childhood, which impact later relationships in the workplace, comes from CEO of The Heim Group and best-selling author, Dr. Pat Heim.

One key insight from their studies was that boys more often – and at earlier ages – participate in team sports, while young girls more often take part in what we refer to as "process play" or "relationship play". These types of activities, things like playing house, nurse, school, etc., don't have a beginning or end, nor a winner or a loser.

In terms of the messages received and lessons learned from these various types of activities, here are a few of their findings:

What we learn from team sports	What we learn from process and relationship play
How to be aggressive	How to share
How to deal with conflict and competition	How to treat others nicely
How to win AND lose	How to avoid conflict
How to be in charge AND how to follow orders when someone else is in charge	How to build and preserve relationships
How to set goals and meet them	How to collaborate
How to play with people we don't like off the field, AND how to compete with people we really do like	How to avoid risks
How to develop game plans, take risks and strategise	How to ensure that everyone has a part

While it's true that girls today play much more team sport than they used to, the men currently in the workplace in their 30s, 40s and 50s probably played many more team sports than their current female colleagues.

The table on the following page highlights some of the impacts that this early gender conditioning (in this *one* particular area, remember) has on male and female workplace behaviours:

Masculine qualities	Feminine qualities
Relationships with peers built through activity	Relationships built through sharing and personal talk
Conflict is seen as maybe necessary	Conflict seen as personal and to be avoided
Task comes first	People come first
Focus on goals	Focus on process
Success due to themselves	Success due to others

It's certainly true for me that I build my relationships through sharing and personal talk. And it's not that men don't bond, they just do it differently – their relationships are glued through activities, which were probably developed because of those team sports. Maybe that's why many team away days are full of activities because that's the way they get close to their male colleagues. If women like to share personal information but men prefer to engage in clay pigeon shooting however are men and women going to be able to build great work relationships? What do you think?

The area of conflict also can't be ignored. It might well be the women who don't like conflict and who want to "fix" things and make everything OK for everyone. But actually, if we let chaos just be for a while, great creativity can break through. And of course we know that great leaders are able to balance the task *and* the people – for without taking care of and motivating the people, no tasks get accomplished.

Re the goal vs. process differences – women and men attack projects and problems differently. Men are more goal-focused while women are more process-focused. Men are more motivated by having a clear goal; and they're highly energised by attaining that goal. The more unattainable, the more motivating it is to get there. Women are more motivated by what goes into the process of getting there – the path to get there is so much more exciting than the actual end itself.

How we attribute success tends to be different for men and women. According to Heim's studies, when men succeed, their natural inclination is to point inward and attribute it to their own skills, talent and hard work. They are not afraid to own their competence. When they fail, they're more likely to point outward. Circumstances outside of their control either caused, or at least contributed to, their failure. Bad timing, bad luck.

Women tend to do the opposite. When we succeed, we point outward. 'I had a great team, I was lucky, I was in the right place at the right time.' We have a very difficult time owning our own competence. When we fail, we point internally. 'I'm not smart enough/I didn't work hard enough.'

Self-Reflection 4

Have you observed or experienced any male/female differences in the area of relationships and how men and women work? Note them.

It's important to stress again that there is no bad or good, and right or wrong about masculine and feminine qualities or about men and women. We all need to be able to draw on the whole range of qualities to use, as situations require. But what *is* true is that whatever the differences actually are, the perceptions of differences play a big part in how we are viewed. Let's look at that now.

Perceptions of differences

Deborah Tannen comments about this in her book *Talking From 9 to 5*. She says:

Individual men or women who speak in ways associated with the other gender will pay a price for departing from cultural expectations.

Women who exhibit masculine qualities like competitiveness and assertiveness and directness can be seen as hard and uncaring. These same qualities would be valued in a man but people don't necessarily like to see them in a woman. Similarly, men who are good listeners and have a more co-operative and consensus style might be seen as lacking in ambition and drive. And women who think they are displaying a positive quality – connection – can be misjudged by men who perceive them to be revealing a lack of independence, which the men regard as synonymous with incompetence and insecurity.

It's the same with networking. Harvard Business School did some research some years ago to look at whether it was true that men networked to build power and influence and women networked to build relationships. Although they found that some women networked to increase power, and some men networked to build relationships, they were viewed quite differently. Men who networked to build relationships weren't seen as credible and women who networked to build influence were seen as manipulative. Seems that we can't win!

Of course, we have no control over how others perceive us but it's good to be aware of what might be going on and how we might be being seen so that we can choose to counter it if we wish. The different perceptions that people may have of men and women at work are summarised brilliantly by Natasha Josefowitz in this poem from her book *Is This Where I Was Going?*

Impressions From An Office

The family picture is on HIS desk
Ah, a solid, responsible family man

The family picture is on HER desk
Umm, her family will come before her career

HIS desk is cluttered	HER desk is cluttered
He's obviously a hard worker and a busy man	She's obviously a disorganised scatterbrain
HE is talking with his co-workers	SHE is talking with her co-workers
He must be discussing the latest deal	She must be gossiping
HE'S not at his desk	SHE'S not at her desk
He must be at a meeting	She must be in the ladies' room
HE'S not in the office	SHE's not in the office
He's meeting customers	She must be out shopping
HE'S having lunch with the boss	SHE'S having lunch with the boss
He's on his way up	They must be having an affair
The boss criticised HIM	The boss criticised HER
He'll improve his performance	She'll be very upset
HE got an unfair deal	SHE got an unfair deal
Did he get angry?	Did she cry?
HE'S getting married	SHE'S getting married
He'll be more settled	She'll get pregnant and leave
HE'S having a baby	SHE'S having a baby
He'll need a rise	She'll cost the company money in maternity benefits
HE'S going on a business trip	SHE'S going on a business trip
It's good for his career	What does her husband say?
HE'S leaving for a better job	SHE'S leaving for a better job
He knows how to recognise a good opportunity	Women are not dependable

So where does all this leave us? Well, firstly, you need to look at where you see yourself in these areas of male/female differences and then look at which qualities you might want to develop in your journey to leadership.

Self-Reflection 5

Is there a particular style (masculine vs. feminine), which is favoured or approved/ disapproved of in your organisation?

If you are working in an organisation which is itself a masculine based one in terms of its operational style and what gets rewarded, and you feel that your feminine strengths are not being recognised or valued, then you have to decide how you are going to stay authentic as you progress into your next leadership role.

We've looked at a lot of differences in masculine and feminine styles and qualities in this chapter so hopefully, as you've been thinking through the self-reflection questions you've been assessing your own style.

Self-Reflection 6

Where do you think your main strengths lie – in a masculine style or a feminine style?

It's all about harmonising the masculine and feminine so let's look at that now.

Harmonising the masculine and feminine

Self-Reflection 7

Out of all the traits that have been detailed – both masculine and feminine – which ones do you want to develop?

Whichever traits you want to develop the idea is to integrate the feminine *and* the masculine inside ourselves. Here are some ways to do that.

First of all let's look at integrating the feminine. There are five things to remember here.

1. Use your empathy, emotions and care, and control your moods. Don't take things personally and don't sound over-emotional.

Not taking things personally is a quality to be employed in our lives in general. It can save us a lot of heartache.

2. Talk about your thoughts and feelings and be more assertive. Give your opinion clearly.

I am always amazed at the numbers of women who are still not able to be assertive. It's a key life skill. It's not the same as aggressive. You have a right to your opinion and you must get used to expressing it in the right way (and that is by respecting other people's rights too). If you feel you are not very assertive then do get some training in this as soon as possible.

3. Use your data gathering and consultation skills and make decisions when they're needed.

Never shy away from making a decision. It's what leaders are paid to do.

4. Continue to be respectful and supportive and take credit for your successes.

Never give away your own credit and make sure the right people know about your successes.

5. Work hard and maintain balance in your life.

Now of course we know that balance is elusive. We have to be flexible – to move this way and that way but always be able to come back to centre for some stillness.

There are a further five things we need to consider when integrating the masculine.

1. Understand the company politics and remain true to your authentic self.

Have the courage to speak out when necessary. This can be very hard but is key to authenticity.

2. Develop your analytical focus and never abandon your empathising skills.

There's room for both and in my experience women can be expert in both these areas.

3. Don't fear conflict, stay compassionate and never get personal.

See conflict as the ebb and flow of life and of decision-making. Conflict is movement and will always lead to resolution at some point.

4. Take charge of your own progression and take your community with you.

Especially other women. You are a role model for other women whether you like it or not. *Every* woman is a role model for every other woman. As you move through your own leadership journey you will be inspiring other women to begin and move through theirs. And as Madeleine Albright (former USA Secretary of State) said: 'There is a special place in hell for women who don't help other women.'

5. Don't be afraid of your own power and remember that the root of your personal power is your authenticity. Never hide it.

You *are* a powerful woman and working from your authentic core people will be inspired by your presence.

Self-Reflection 8

Where do you think you add value to your organisation *because* you are a woman?

The great leader can use both masculine and feminine skills to do a truly outstanding job. Developing your own leadership style takes time and a lot of self-reflection. Don't neglect this aspect of your leadership journey.

Chapter 3

The Concept of Authenticity

Authenticity is referenced as an essential quality for leaders. But what exactly does it mean? Is authenticity really essential for leadership? And can people be trained to be authentic?

In this chapter:

- ► Different perspectives on authenticity
- ► Authenticity and leadership
- ► Is authenticity different for women and men?
- ► Authenticity as a journey

Different perspectives on authenticity

I once posted a question on one of the discussion groups on LinkedIn:

Can you train people to be authentic?

There seems to be general agreement that authenticity is a desirable even necessary quality for a leader. But how do we learn to be authentic? Is it something we can train leaders in? And how do we measure it?

I was interested to know what others thought about this whole idea of authenticity. It is a much-used word at the moment to the extent that it seems to have no meaning at all. There were 78 comments and 21 people took part in the discussion. I know this is a very small sample but people made some very interesting points. Here is a selection of some of the common threads that came out:

1. Authenticity isn't just for leaders – it's for everyone.

2. One can learn to be authentic through a process of self-discovery and increased self-awareness.

3. Authenticity lies in the synthesis of head and heart.

4. Maybe you can't train people to be authentic but you can develop them through coaching.

5. If you have to learn to be authentic then you are creating a fake!

6. Our authenticity will be tied to our beliefs and values – the journey lies in uncovering those and acting in line with what we perceive as our own truth.

7. Maybe we underestimate how hard it is to be authentic.

8. For authenticity to flourish in organisations there needs to be role modelling at all levels and authentic behaviour rewarded.

9. You can't force people to be authentic – they have to be willing to engage in the journey and discover it in themselves, not learn to dress up in it.

10. Developing authenticity is about enabling and encouraging personal transformation.

I'm not going to comment on these individual statements but I do want you to think about them. Remember that this is one of the Concept chapters to help you to think through some important issues in your own journey to leadership.

Self-Reflection 1

What do you think authenticity is?

You will see that the comments above range from authenticity being linked to values and the importance of the journey towards authenticity, to the idea that creating an authentic person is, by definition, fake: you're either real or you're not.

What was perhaps more interesting were the questions raised by the discussion. Let's have a look at those:

1. Is authenticity different from other qualities we expect leaders to have?

We expect leaders to have integrity; to be loyal; to have charisma so they can inspire; to have communication skills; to have courage and determination; to have know-how; to have a vision – of something better; to have insight and initiative; to have impact; to be able to influence and to manage ambiguity. So is authenticity something different to these?

2. If authenticity is being true to oneself – what "self" are we being true to?

Here the question was raised of where authenticity lies within us. Is it a necessary part of our ego; the part of us that has to function well in this world and to always have an eye on the outputs and gains? Or does authenticity lie in our Best Self; the part of us that is untainted by worldly and material concerns so that, as leaders, we can bring out the Best Selves in our teams and collectively create better visions and ultimately better world?

3. Is developing authenticity a personal responsibility or an organisational one?

There were many comments about how exactly we are supposed to develop our authenticity muscle. Is it merely a personal journey of self-development or is there an organisational responsibility to provide the environment where authenticity can flourish, and provide the space for leaders to get in touch with this deeper part of themselves?

Then there is the question about great leaders:

4. Can you be a great leader yet not be authentic?

These people are often quoted as being great leaders: Alexander the Great, the Duke of Wellington, Sir Winston Churchill, Gandhi, Martin Luther King Jr., John F. Kennedy and more recently Steve Jobs. History is littered with men like these (and it's usually men who make the list of great leaders) who had deep personal flaws. But when you read their biographies it is obvious that they all share a common trait: a belief in themselves that transcended contradiction and reality.

So maybe those we perceive as the "greatest" leaders are frequently flawed – does that mean they are not authentic? If we study charismatic leadership we can see a marked reluctance of historically recognised great leaders to accept from any other vision but their own. This lack of ability to compromise was in most cases the cause of their downfall. So how strong *is* that link between authenticity and leadership?

Question 5 seeks to shed some light on this:

5. Can you divorce authenticity from the situation where it is needed and can be seen?

Maybe there is no such thing as great leaders, just great events when exactly the right person is in place to harness the energy and do the most good. Churchill was hailed as a hero and leader and instrumental in defeating Hitler, yet he was in the wilderness and derided for almost 20 years before his moment in history turned up.

So does authenticity always have to concern itself with the greater good? This is the next question:

6. Does being authentic always involve acting for the greater good, beyond personal desires and ego?

If we believe that authenticity is about being true to ourselves all of the time then we could be accused of exhibiting narcissistic behaviours that deny others a say in our reality. Should we sometimes be true to others, or the community as a whole rather than the self? Of course this would necessitate that a leader had a high degree of intelligent self-awareness and could judge if it was right at that particular time to be not true to oneself but to be true to the wider group. Maybe the case is that when a situation is called for that needs drastic change, the energy needed to be the catalyst for it will naturally rise to the surface. That it isn't about the person, it's about the timing and the individual allowing themselves to be the conduit for something greater than themselves.

7. What is the point of being authentic? Is it to know ourselves so we enter life's interactions and relationships from a more honest place? Or is it to be better leaders?

I would argue that these two things are intertwined. Self-awareness is critical for authenticity, for unless we know ourselves, our values, and our flaws, how can we even measure for ourselves and check that we are meeting our own standards? Self-awareness is also critical for leaders who are carrying a vision and tasked to inspire those who work for them. And anyway, we are *all* leaders aren't we? We are leaders of our own lives; we are role models for everyone who sees us.

So can we choose *not* to be authentic? Question 8 asks this:

8. Is it OK to choose to hide some things about ourselves in certain situations and is that being socially and emotionally intelligent or is that being inauthentic?

Maybe there are aspects of us all that are appropriate to different places and circumstances and it's important to offer the right perspective and aspect to correspond to each situation. It's not about trying to hide who or what we are but to use discretion as to how much we open up personally and with whom.

Maybe authenticity is a social ability. Implicit in the concept of being authentic — "being actually what is claimed" — are qualities of interactive behavior. We regard a person as authentic to the extent that her conduct towards others accords with what she truly believes in. Authenticity, then, is about giving a message about your true self — one you must continually shape and deliver by thoughtfully choosing your words and behaviours to suit the people you interact with and the specific purpose at hand. This isn't being inauthentic; it's being socially skilled.

Finally, maybe the crux of the whole matter:

9. Do we all have an authentic core waiting to be uncovered and discovered or is it possible to build an authentic core from ideas and philosophies?

We have to decide for ourselves: do we believe we have an authentic core; it's just that we need to uncover it? Or can we start from scratch and learn, study and adopt ideas and philosophies then implant them, as it were, inside us? What exactly *is* our journey to authenticity?

Before answering that I want to share with you a summary of what I believe are the components of authentic leadership. There are three main areas.

SELF-IDENTITY: self-awareness, self-esteem, self-knowledge, self-concept, and personal mastery of emotions.

It seems that self-awareness is particularly important. Of all the things I have read and heard about leadership, it is self-awareness that is mentioned most often.

But there are another two things to add into the self-awareness pot: self-esteem and emotional intelligence (which is personal mastery of the emotions). Self-esteem is not just a nice thing to have; it is critical for sustained high performance. We saw back in Chapter 1 the three main reasons why women don't have high self-esteem – do you remember? Feeling that they don't have a voice, not being inclined to challenge the status quo and not fitting in.

Self-knowledge includes knowing our values and beliefs and knowing our shadow spots; the things that trip us up and fling us back into jealousies or worry or guilt – the things that put the brake on our performance.

Emotional intelligence is now recognised as being needed by all of us, not only leaders, who want good relationships and partnerships whether in our personal lives or in business. We'll talk about self-awareness more when we look at authenticity as a journey in the next section.

LEADER IDENTITY: highly developed sense of their leader role and responsibility to act morally and in the best interests of others, including accepting fully the consequences of their decisions.

This includes all the usual expectations of leaders that we mentioned already but now we add in the idea of responsibility to have the interests of *everyone* at heart – not just self or team or even organisation but also the wider society, the environment, the planet. We all know that the very stuff of leadership is making choices and making decisions but it also takes immense courage to take responsibility for those decisions. Yet this is essential.

SPIRITUAL IDENTITY: inner life, meaning and purpose shown through self-disclosure, self-transcendence and self-sacrifice.

Part of being true to ourselves is really knowing who we are at our core. What is our meaning and purpose in life? And how does our work help or hinder that purpose? This question is so important that we will be looking at it in detail in the last chapter of this book.

How is our Spiritual Identity seen? Through self-disclosure, which is allowing ourselves to be seen as vulnerable and enables others to accept us in all our humanness. That very acceptance increases our self-esteem. It's also seen through self-transcendance, which is about integrating all the aspects of ourselves – physical, emotional, mental and spiritual – and being able to adopt an integrated and holistic perspective. And through self-sacrifice, which is about our ability to sometimes sacrifice our own needs for the higher good, the good of the team, and a willingness to speak out maybe even at the cost of losing our job.

Self-Reflection 2

Which of these components of authentic leadership do you think you need to develop the most? How will you do that?

Authenticity and leadership

When we are looking at authenticity and leadership I would suggest there are two more things to consider. One would be: working for the highest good for all. Some leaders are charismatic and inspirational and many follow them. But do they work for the highest good of all? Where was Steve Jobs' "highest good for all"? And who is the "all"? Stakeholders? Shareholders? Customers? Employees? Jobs didn't have the best reputation on a personal level but does revolutionising how our world works, and building a multi-billion dollar business make him a great leader despite that? And aren't there people whose vision and purpose are seriously flawed? They might be true to their own beliefs but are they great leaders?

I want my leaders (in whatever capacity they are leading) to have a bigger vision than their own tiny world. And I want them to be committed to their own development so their own purpose can be aligned with a higher one, which serves a bigger section of humanity than the small segment they might actually be responsible for.

The second thing I see as necessary is sustainability. Churchill stepped up in a crisis and had the courage to do what was needed, when it was needed. But when the crisis was over his party lost the election and ultimately the people rejected him. Maybe there are some people who are perfect leaders only in a particular set of circumstances. When we talk of developing leaders we mean in general I think. We don't want to just see flashes – we want consistency so we will trust him/her. And while some mistakes might be forgiven (Bill Clinton is still hugely regarded in spite of his personal failings), others won't be. I don't think a large section of the British people will ever forgive Tony Blair for the way he took the UK into war. Was/ is he authentic? He was certainly true to himself. But would I ever trust the wisdom of his judgements again? No I wouldn't.

So are there any guidelines to help us to become the best authentic leaders we can be? In 2007, Bill George, Pete Sims, Andrew N. McLean and Diana Mayer carried out research into leadership – *Discovering Your Authentic Leadership* – published by Harvard Business Review.

We interviewed 125 leaders to learn how they developed their leadership abilities. These interviews constitute the largest in-depth study of leadership development ever undertaken. Our interviewees discussed openly and honestly how they realised their potential and candidly shared their life stories, personal struggles, failures, and triumphs.

The people we talked with ranged in age from 23 to 93, with no fewer than 15 per decade. They were chosen based on their reputations for authenticity and effectiveness as leaders, as well as our personal knowledge of them. We also solicited recommendations from other leaders and academics. The resulting group includes women and men from a diverse array of racial, religious, and socioeconomic backgrounds and nationalities. Half of them are CEOs, and the other half comprises a range of profit and nonprofit leaders, midcareer leaders, and young leaders just starting on their journeys.

I think their findings are still pertinent. After 3000 pages of transcripts they saw that there was no magic formula for creating a great leader and no definitive list of characteristics we can all seek to develop. Their greatest finding was that:

Discovering your authentic leadership requires a commitment to developing yourself.

They were able to come up with some guidelines as to how one could do that which I'd like to share with you.

1. Learn from your life story.

The journey to authentic leadership begins with understanding the story of your life. Your life story provides the context for your experiences, and through it, you can find the inspiration to make an impact in the world. The leaders interviewed traced their inspiration directly from their life stories.

Asked what empowered them to lead, these leaders consistently replied that they found their strength through the transformative experiences they had had in their lives. Those experiences enabled them to understand the deeper purpose of their leadership. Do start to think about your life story now and the lessons you have learned. It's the start for defining meaning and purpose in your life.

2. Practise your values.

It is relatively easy to list your values and to live by them when things are going well. When your success, your career, or even your life hangs in the balance, you learn what is most important, what you are prepared to sacrifice, and what trade-offs you are willing to make. We mentioned this already in self-sacrifice when we were talking about Spiritual Identity.

Leadership principles are values translated into action. Having a solid base of values and testing them under fire enables you to develop the principles you will use in leading. For example, a value such as "concern for others" might be translated into a leadership principle such as: 'Create a work environment where people are respected for their contributions, provided job security, and allowed to fulfil their potential.'

3. Understand what drives you.

There are two types of motivations – extrinsic and intrinsic. Many leaders seek success in the outside, material world. They enjoy the recognition and status that come with promotions and financial rewards. Intrinsic motivations, on the other hand, are derived from their sense of the meaning of their life. They are closely linked to one's life story and the way one frames it. Examples include personal growth, helping other people develop, taking on social causes, and making a difference in the world. The key is to find a balance between your desires for external validation and the intrinsic motivations that provide fulfilment in your work.

4. Build your support team.

Authentic leaders build extraordinary support teams to help them stay on course. Those teams counsel them in times of uncertainty, help them in times of difficulty, and celebrate with them in times of success. After their hardest days, leaders find comfort in being with people on whom they can rely so they can be open and vulnerable. During the low points, they cherish the friends who appreciate them for who they are, not what they are. Authentic leaders find that their support teams provide affirmation, advice, perspective, and call for course corrections when needed.

5. Integrate yourself; integrate your life.

To lead a balanced life, you need to bring together all of its constituent elements – work, family, community, friends – so that you can be the same person in each environment. Being authentic means maintaining a sense of self no matter where you are. Authentic leaders have a steady and confident presence. They do not show up as one person one day and another person the next. Integration takes discipline, particularly during stressful times when it is easy to become reactive and slip back into bad habits.

Authentic leaders are constantly aware of the importance of staying grounded and integrating *all* aspects of self. Besides spending time with their families and close friends, authentic leaders get physical exercise, engage in spiritual practices, do community service, and return to the places where they grew up. They are also capable of showing affection and laughing and having fun.

All these things are essential to their effectiveness as leaders, enabling them to sustain their authenticity.

Leading is high-stress work. There is no way to avoid stress when you are responsible for people, organisations, outcomes, and managing the constant uncertainties of the environment. The higher you go, the greater your freedom to control your destiny but also the higher the degree of stress. The question is not whether you can avoid stress but how you can control it to maintain your own sense of equilibrium. We will look at stress in more depth later in the book.

Is authenticity different for women than for men?

Finally, let's look at whether there is a gender angle here. I think the difference is in the journey. If authenticity is about knowing, and being, who you truly are, then I do think women have a harder time discovering their sense of self. One of the reasons is because of all the roles we play in our lives.

Many of these roles have been decided by societal patterns, which were largely defined by men. Women who try to step out of a defined role – whether that be wanting to train as a pilot, or wanting to work and have children, or choosing not to have children, or demonstrating directness and assertiveness – have paid the price for stepping over the boundary; a boundary that someone else has set up for them. Of course, society patterns are changing all the time but for women caught in the transition process it can be painful. We have to discover who we are *behind* our roles.

We can see the results in the lack of self-esteem that many women suffer from. So for women, really understanding yourself and knowing yourself means that we have to understand where we came from. What are the things that bind us and stop us being who we truly are?

Then there is the issue of working in a masculine environment or organisational culture and feeling out of place. There aren't enough women leaders yet for people to realise that each one is individual (which is how people see male leaders). So women are viewed collectively.

The attributes and behaviours that are deemed assets for male leaders are considered unnatural and unattractive in women. A man who is assertive and takes control is admired; a woman who acts the same way is not. Extensive research has established that women are judged as either likeable or competent, but not both. When they act in ways that appear feminine (e.g. collaborative, supportive) they may be liked but they are not respected as competent leaders. When their behaviour is more masculine (e.g. autonomous, authoritative), they may be seen as competent but they are not liked. Even when women are rated higher than men in specific leadership competencies, they are rated lower in leadership potential.

Women respond to this environment in many ways. Here are some examples.

Some women:

- Use a masculine style. For example, they may become overbearing and autocratic to prove they can be tough
- Downplay their femininity. They are "all business" and conceal their "softer" side
- Avoid self-promotion because it seems too much like bragging, which is considered unfeminine
- Are restrained when negotiating on their own behalf, even though they are superb negotiators for their clients
- Resist networking because it seems too much like "using people" for your own ends
- Avoid wielding power when they have it – or fail to recognise the power they have
- Avoid situations where their leadership style might be visible (e.g. decision making, delegating work)

These responses may make women feel comfortable in a difficult work environment, but they can derail a promising career. Most of these responses are not just expedient; they are inauthentic. They do not necessarily reflect who a woman is naturally, but represent coping behaviours that are less risky and easier to use. But they also lead to lack of trust and credibility among colleagues.

Because women are not sure how they "should" behave as leaders, they become preoccupied about how they appear to others rather than concentrating on their own values and what they want to accomplish. Consequently they focus too much on meeting others' expectations and on creating the "right" leadership image for others. This saps them of energy, creates constant frustration, and detracts from their purpose as leaders.

So, as well as self-esteem, I think women require more courage and determination than men may do in their journey to being an authentic leader. I also think they need to be more socially skilled to recognise the situations they are in and choose the most appropriate style for the situation, as long as they are still in tune with their needs and comfortable in their own skin. The world of business is not going to change overnight so women need to weave their way through it to remain tuned to themselves as well as delivering on leadership demands.

Finding one's inner self – one's "beingness" – where our authenticity lies, is like learning to ride a bicycle. It starts out being difficult but after time and practice it feels a bit more natural. It takes time for women because we have assumed identities based on our roles. This is why some women, when marriages fall apart or children leave home are left feeling so disconnected. Apart from the understandable feelings of loss there is a sense of futileness – who am I now?

But once we begin to live an authentic life our actions will follow our words. We'll live from the heart as well as the head. And we'll connect with our Spirit. And when we allow our heart and our Spirit to be our drivers instead of our roles and other people's expectations of us, then we will find our centre, our essence, our beingness – our true identity. Authenticity isn't something to dress up in – it's allowing our essence to shine through.

We can change our lives by discovering who we are – and by changing our lives, I believe we can change the world.

Self-Reflection 3

Do you think the issues for men and women are different regarding authenticity? What is your greatest struggle in finding and operating from your authentic self?

Authenticity as a journey

I see the journey to authenticity as being a journey to the centre of the Self. I think that our authentic self is linked to our Best Self – our highest self, which is already in us somewhere. The leadership journey is to find the path back to it whether that is via a physical, emotional, mental or spiritual route. If leadership is about "being" more than "doing" then surely we have to get as close as we can to that "being" and operate from there. So the journey *will* be about self-discovery and self-awareness.

On a leadership programme I ran there was a very senior woman from a global corporation based in Australia who said that she hadn't taken time out to think exclusively about herself for seven years. If we are to know ourselves then we *must* allow time for self-reflection, reading, rumination and examination.

And I think that organisations have a role to play here. We all have a personal responsibility to organise our own lives, priorities and lifestyles. But when people are spending more hours at work than they do at home and their work becomes their life, and organisations encourage people to "bring your whole self to work" then I think organisations *do* have a responsibility to play their part in giving people space to look at their "wholeness", if for no other reason than to get the optimum performance out of them.

When we are doing our jobs and managing a busy schedule we need to be able to find our own inner balance amid the seeming chaos and set aside the time to put together a strategy for finding and maintaining inner balance. Accessing and bringing forward the authentic self deserves a place that I see as equally important as setting aside the time to discuss a marketing strategy or a sales strategy.

And, for the record, I'm not a believer in the school of thought that says that you are authentic or you're not, and if you're not, you never can be! I believe that a leopard *can* change its spots. The more self-aware we become and the more we commit to our self-discovery the more we can *choose* to change those spots.

Yet, if we believe that authenticity comes from within then is there an assumption that we all have an authentic self, it's just that many of us can't access it or are unwilling to show it? In which case, developing authenticity has to be about becoming self-aware enough to identify the blocks to our authenticity and then having the dedication to remove the blocks, and courage to show and express our authenticity.

I also believe it's about transcending our lower nature and growing into our full potential as human beings and I think it's the most important and the most fulfilling thing any of us can do with our lives. Yet, although we might be drawn towards our own higher potential, we quickly see that not only are there a variety of names for this journey (self-actualisation, spiritual awakening, personal transformation) but there also seems to be a variety of paths we can follow. Our journey is to find our way through this maze, to become spiritually intelligent and authentic leaders. Cindy Wigglesworth describes Spiritual Intelligence as: *'The ability to behave with wisdom and compassion while maintaining inner and outer peace, regardless of the situation.'* She has defined 21 skills of Spiritual Intelligence each with five competence levels and an online assessment tool to assess your skill level. It's worth looking at Cindy's SQ21 to see if her model can be of any help to you in your own journey.

As for personal integration (of our ego-driven self with our higher or best self), I think it is a slow process that takes willingness to recognise our ego-centred behaviours and courage to eliminate them. Self-awareness, determination, courage – all of these are necessary for the authentic self to be revealed.

I believe that authenticity lives at the level of the soul and at that level there is no differentiation, only unity. I believe that once we get to the level of soul then we cannot help but be, not only concerned about, but also connected to the bigger picture and what is best for all. To unlock the door to our authenticity we have to be prepared to do the work on clearing the blockages on the emotional and mental levels or we don't have a clean "vessel" to express our authenticity through.

When I use the word "authentic" there is an underlying assumption (from me) that when applied to a leader it refers to someone who *is* self-aware, who can see beyond their own ego, who is willing to work on themselves (and take time for themselves) and has at least a smattering of wisdom and discernment. So someone who is being very "real" and "true to themselves" but is basically a jerk wouldn't cut it.

Finally, babies don't have low self-esteem – they learn that from their environment and people around them who shape them. So I see the journey to authenticity to consist of doing anything we can so we can return to our real, confident, fearless, authentic selves.

These are my views. There are many who might disagree with me. The purpose of these first chapters on exploring concepts – and especially this chapter on authenticity – is to give you food for thought. You have to consider carefully your own ideas about authenticity, who you want to be as an authentic leader and how you are going to get there.

Self-Reflection 4

Is there anything specifically you want to focus on at this point of your journey to authenticity?

Part 2
Overcoming Obstacles

Chapter 4

Removing Internal Barriers

Do you know what unconscious internal barriers are preventing you from progressing? And if you are aware, do you know how to overcome them? It might seem odd to be focusing on what's wrong with our thinking but some of the ideas and beliefs we hold about ourselves are so deeply ingrained that we are hardly aware of how powerful they are in driving our actions. We're going to look at 10 barriers that can stop you from accessing your authentic power. Think about each of the barriers very carefully and really assess where they might have played out in your life. Consider the price you're paying while these barriers are in place, and what strategies you can put in place to help to remove them.

Barrier 1 – *'I couldn't possibly…'*

Think how many times you have turned down opportunities because you say to yourself: 'I'd love that job but I couldn't possibly…' or 'I'd really like to train for that but… I probably wouldn't get accepted'. It's the "buts" of this world that prevent people from succeeding. They impose limits on their capabilities and restrict their potential. As we saw in Chapter 2 on male and female differences, women, in particular, tend to emphasise their weaknesses and undermine their strengths. This can become a self-fulfilling prophecy, and what's more, people might start to believe them. When things are going well they put it down to luck or other people. When things are going badly they feel guilty and accept the blame far too readily. This leads to a loss of self-esteem and confirms the views that people might already have of women – that women are good at some things and not at others. But the result of this is that these women won't put themselves forward when opportunities arise. From the stories I have heard directly (and there is research to back this up) a man will look at a job description and might see that there is 15% of it he can't do. He will think to himself, 'I can do 85% of that and I'll learn the rest on the job. No problem.' A woman seeing the same job description and also realising she can do 85% of it *will see only the 15% she can't do*, and probably won't even bother to apply.

In fact, there is no limit to what you can achieve if you put your mind to it.

Sometimes this barrier is because we believe we don't have the authority to say and act in a particular way. So if you don't have a lot of position power you might be intimidated by those in positions of authority, feeling that you are inferior in comparison. If you see yourself in the role of helper, supporter and even fixer, then it's easier sometimes to carry on doing this. But it's also easier for others to continue to see you in a supporting role instead of a leadership role. It's important to take responsibility for your own progress and not be afraid of acquiring external power. And meanwhile continue to work on realising your authentic power, which is your real power base.

Self-Reflection 1

Did you ever hold back from a job opportunity or doing something you really wanted to do because you thought 'I couldn't possibly…'? Do you speak about your weaknesses more than your strengths?

Removing this barrier

- Look at what you *can* do; not what you can't
- Appraise your skills realistically
- Never attribute your success to "luck"
- Stop making negative statements about yourself
- Stop yourself talking about your weaknesses
- Talk more about your strengths

Barrier 2 – *'I don't want to be an authority figure.'*

Women sometimes have a problem with authority because we see it as authority *over* someone and we might have been many times in the position of the person on the receiving end of someone's abuse of authority. We don't want to be like that. We don't want to treat people badly. We know what it is like to be the "less than" so we steer away from a position that might make us the person in authority. It's true that being in authority means that we do have to take control in some situations but this doesn't mean being an autocrat or a bully. We will be expected to solve problems and make decisions, take responsibility and be accountable to someone else. To run anything well you have to take charge, and there are some women who hold back from this.

But suppose we saw authority as an opportunity to empower people who work for us and enable everyone to do their best work? We need to welcome authority and learn how to use it well. It doesn't mean we have to browbeat others in order to do the job. There are ways of handling authority that can make the job easier and more pleasant for all concerned. Women have picked up many skills in their life experiences around getting the best out of people – raising children, managing family care situations, running voluntary activities in the community. Maybe if we saw our workplaces as communities we would be more comfortable managing them with ease.

We are not used to seeing ourselves as authority figures and from our experience of being on the receiving end of authority we're not sure we want it either. So let's start to see authority differently and as a positive way to bring about change. We can practise by taking charge of our own lives. We are the best authority on ourselves and by learning to be in control of what we do by making choices and accepting responsibility for the consequences, we will start to become confident and sure about the power that authority brings.

Sometimes we have a reluctance to be an authority figure because we don't want to be seen as "pushy". Some men, and some women, might describe women who have position power as "pushy". This is often because some of the qualities that are seen as desirable in a man are seen as unacceptable in a woman. And sometimes it is because some women adopt an aggressive mode because they think that is the only way to succeed.

Speaking up for yourself, speaking out at meetings, not allowing yourself to be interrupted... these are not aggressive traits – these are assertive traits and they are absolutely necessary as you move into a leadership role. If you are assertive you might well be seen as "pushy" but remember: you have no control over how other people think of you so it's no use trying to tailor your behaviour to suit everyone – it's unrealistic and impossible. So make sure you are assertive, not aggressive, and give others permission to think what they like. That's not your business; it's theirs.

Self-Reflection 2

Did you ever hold back from saying something or doing something because you didn't think it was your place? How comfortable are you with the idea of being in a position of authority? Have you ever been described as "pushy"?
Why do you think this was?

Removing this barrier

- Clearly define for yourself the difference between authority and leadership
- Identify the leadership values you want to live by
- Be clear about the differences between assertive and aggressive behaviour
- Get assertiveness training if you need it or look up "assertiveness at work" for lots of free resources and help

Barrier 3 – *'Let's get it just right.'*

We can also call this the perfection block. This is about endless fiddling with things to get them just right. We start when we are girls in school. I used to be a schoolteacher of pupils aged 11-16 and I could look at work handed in and put it into two piles – girls and boys – without looking at the names. The girls' work would (usually) be beautifully presented; pages decorated, different coloured pens used, neat underlining, no crossings out... while the boys' work would be hastily scribbled with no decoration at all. This is a generalisation: it doesn't apply to all girls and all boys, but it does apply to enough for it to be noticeable.

If presentation is going to be awarded marks then the girls are going to do well but if the content is all that gets assessed then the girls have wasted precious time.

Sometimes we do this at home too. We delegate cleaning the bathroom to one of our children and then go in and redo it because they haven't done it to our standards. So we either haven't given clear enough directions about the standards for the job, or we should make them do it again, and again, until they do it right. You can't delegate to children and then move in and take over; you might as well do it yourself in the first place if you are going to do that.

Now fast-forward to the workplace. How many women do a piece of work and then fiddle with it; add to it, change bits of it, make it look pretty... all of which is time spent on something that is actually finished instead of moving on to the next thing to be done.

The higher up the scale you go at work, the more you are likely to have an admin assistant whose job it is to lay it out nicely and make it look pretty so we have to learn to focus on what is important not what satisfies our innate desire for creating a pleasing appearance. Not everything worth doing is worth doing well: some things are just worth doing and getting rid of!

We even do this when looking at our careers. We feel we have to do one job perfectly before we can think of seeking the next rung up the ladder. Ambitious men think differently. In mapping out a career path, men work at their present job while keeping an eye on what they need to do for the next one. In contrast, some women become obsessed with perfect standards and then are overtaken when it comes to promotion.

Self-Reflection 3

Do you think you have a "perfection" block?
How does it get played out at work? And at home?

Removing this barrier

- Monitor yourself to see how often you keep revisiting a completed task to see if you can improve it

- Write out on a sticky note: 'Not everything worth doing is worth doing well' and put it where you can see it regularly

- Anytime you feel guilty about not doing something exactly right tell yourself: 'I'm doing the best that I can, and it's good enough.'

Barrier 4 – *'Let's be one happy family.'*

As women we have learned to be the peacemakers. We are the peacemakers between our children, between our children and our husband, between other family members. We want everything to be happy and nice (that's the way we were brought up as girls remember?) So we have a desire to fix things.

As mothers we are Queen Fixers. We make things better. We kiss better sore knees; we hug our daughter when her best friend falls out with her; we organise the annual get-togethers; we sit up all night with a sick child... Nothing wrong with any of this but we shouldn't necessarily be operating like this in the workplace.

Sometimes, at work, we have to let chaos and conflict just "be" because out of that can come great creativity. Of course we have to move in if someone is being damaged (discrimination, bullying, harassment) but if we are talking about conflict when working on a project then let's get comfortable with it and not move in too soon just because we are uncomfortable. Let's always assess what is best for the situation.

We have to remember that it's not our job to fix people. We can offer help and advice but people have to fix themselves. They are the only ones who can do it, and we don't do them a service by trying to do it for them. If we are constantly trying to fix everyone's problems then that is how we will be seen. 'Go to Anne – she'll sort you out.' So here are you, Anne, sorting out another problem, which is nothing to do with you, while what exactly happens to your work?

Our gender might also have impacted on our desire to be open. We are often honest and trusting in our personal relationships, especially with our female friends, and find it much easier to be open than men would be with their male friends. But being open is not always the best policy at work. Revealing one's fears and faults can create empathy and understanding among friends but at work may be seen as a lack of confidence and even cause people to lose respect for us. Being totally honest all the time, particularly about our weaknesses, can put women at a disadvantage, as power often comes to those who keep silent about their vulnerabilities.

Self-Reflection 4

Have you ever been seen as a mother or sister or sympathetic ear and given time to people at the expense of your work? How comfortable are you with tension and/or chaos in the team?

Removing this barrier

- Don't allow yourself to be interrupted by people wanting to talk personally with you – arrange a specific time to see them when it's convenient for you
- Next time there is a disagreement in the team hold yourself back from moving in straightaway to fix it

Barrier 5 – *'Someone will notice soon.'*

D oes this sound familiar? We do a great job, we know it's a great job, so we wait for others to recognise what a great job we've done and tell us. Well maybe they will – but maybe they won't! While we want credit for what we've done we don't like to bring attention to it. We think that by being loyal, conscientious and good at our jobs we will be automatically rewarded with promotion. Not necessarily!

We have to let people know what we have done and bring it to their attention (as in the people who matter, like our boss). I know of women who have worked on something with a male colleague, and together they have produced a report. However, when the report gets published and circulated she sees that her name doesn't appear on it. And there are women who produce some creative, innovative ideas and share them but nothing seems to happen with them. Until she sees them appear with someone else's name attached to them.

If you do a good piece of work you need to make sure that your name is attached to it, and you have to let people know what you have done. No one should be more invested in your credibility and reputation than you, so you have to take control of it.

I remember talking to a group of women on a workshop. The conversation went something like this:

Them: *There is a young man who has joined our team and every five minutes it seems he is down in the boss's office and we have so much work to do in this department...*

Me: *So what happens to his work while he is talking with the boss?*

Them: *Well, we have to do it.*

Me: *No, you don't have to do it. Clearly you are doing it but you don't have to. More importantly, why aren't you in the boss's office telling him about your ideas?*

Them: *We wouldn't dream of just walking into the boss's office giving him ideas and suggestions without being asked.*

Me: *So here is what's going to happen. You will carry on doing your work, and your male colleague's work, while he is talking ideas with the boss. Then in a few months* *when a new opportunity comes up in the organisation the boss will be saying, 'Hey – I have a young guy in my team who would be perfect. He's full of good ideas and creative solutions.' And your colleague will move on and up – and you will still be here doing your reports...*

If you want to be noticed for your good work then you have to bring your good work to the attention of those who matter. As women, we are not very good at doing this. We don't like drawing attention to ourselves, and we have to change that and celebrate our successes.

Self-Reflection 5

Did someone else ever get credit for your work? How did you feel?
What did you do about it?

Removing this barrier

- Ensure your name is on every piece of work you do
- Tell at least two people at work this week about something great you have done
- At every meeting with your manager make sure s/he knows about something you have achieved since the last time you met or spoke

Barrier 6 – *'I'm frightened of power/success.'*

Maybe you have ambivalent feelings towards promotion because you fear the power and success associated with it, even though you would like the responsibility, interest and benefits of the job.

You may harbour such feelings for a number of reasons:

- You might fear not being liked
- You will be uncomfortable being in a more senior position than your current colleagues and friends
- You are worried about making wrong decisions
- You fear you might not be able to maintain the standard expected of you
- You fear you might let down those who appointed you
- You don't know how to handle certain people
- You can't see yourself coping with the demands of the job

All these beliefs that women have about themselves arise from a lack of self-confidence but by the time you have finished working through the OPAL way in this book your confidence and your self-esteem will be greatly increased, and the door to your authentic power wide open.

Remember: you have to assess "success" realistically in terms of the benefits that it can bring to your life. If you want the power to influence and change things, then you have to seize all opportunities that you get to sit in the hot seat.

Self-Reflection 6

What fears do you have about future success?
Do you think these fears are holding you back?

Removing this barrier

- Read *Feel the Fear and Do It Anyway* by Susan Jeffers
- Worrying about things beyond your control is wasted time. When you find yourself worrying take 10 deep breaths and think of five things to be grateful for right now
- Write down all the things you have achieved in your life that you are proud of and look at it whenever you doubt yourself

Barrier 7 – *'I don't feel as if I've achieved much.'*

As women, we are used to producing results. We produce dinners, children, Christmas, Thanksgiving, clean washing, family holidays... We are used to seeing a result of what we do. So let's credit ourselves firstly for all the results we do achieve in these areas. But let's remember that at work, sometimes what is required of us is our ideas, our project management, our delegation skills, our creativity, our innovation – things that don't have immediate visible results. Yet thinking, planning, discussing and socialising are productive leadership tasks and need to be recognised as such.

How many of us look at our desk at 3pm and say: 'Oh my goodness look at the time – what I have done today for goodness sake...' Well, maybe you were thinking and planning about something that will come to fruition in the next six months. And that's fine. It's a result too. So instead of looking at our daily list and seeing that there is hardly anything crossed off let's look instead at who we empowered today, how someone or the organisation will benefit from what we have spent 2-3 hours doing. The higher up the ladder we go, the more we are being paid for our thoughts, our vision and our strategy so let's not be blocked by our inner drive to produce. Let's also acknowledge our more abstract offerings as things we *can* do.

Self-Reflection 7

What activities have you done in the last week that will show results in the future but not immediately? When do you get tempted to work on less important things so that you can feel you have done something?

Removing this barrier

- Sort out your tasks into important and urgent and make sure you do some important ones every day
- Do at least one thing every day that is related to long-term benefits as opposed to short-term fire fighting
- Delegate more – especially the less important tasks

Barrier 8 – *'I'm not very ambitious.'*

Being ambitious doesn't mean that you have to aim for the very top of the tree. Much will depend on your personal values and circumstances. And it doesn't mean that you have to sacrifice all the interests and people in your life. Many women, and many men, have learned, to their cost, the consequences of a life that is exclusively centred on work and work-related issues. Being ambitious is about choosing your goal, and making the most of your talents, your potential and your life. Being ambitious is about being in control of your life and your career and carving out a path.

Linked to this barrier sometimes is the idea that if you really go for the career and the job you want then you will need to adopt a competitive attitude which you don't always feel comfortable with. Competing with another company for market share of a product is one thing but competing with another individual for a job is quite another. Sometimes women find themselves in a double bind. If they "win" they fear humiliating the other party – the relationship becomes more important than the event and we know what losing feels like; if they lose this just confirms any feelings of inadequacy they have. To be comfortable with competing, and so that we don't put the brakes on our ambition, we need to not be held back by thoughts of winning and losing. The important thing is to be "in the game" and developing the skills to keep you in the running.

And risk-taking is an element of competing and ambition, which has to be faced and even sought. If you lose, you learn from your mistakes and carry on, thus increasing your personal strengths; there will be plenty more opportunities. If you win, enjoy it. There is no growth – or advancement – without risk.

Self-Reflection 8

Would you describe yourself as ambitious? As competitive? Have you ever been held back by your attitude to competing, or winning and losing?

Removing this barrier

- Write down the next job you want
- Write down the job you want after that job!
- Update your CV and include *all* your skills

Barrier 9 – *'I'll see what the organisation has in mind for me.'*

If you want to be responsible for others, you have to start by assuming responsibility for yourself. Although many organisations have an established promotion process, you might need certain experience before going for certain jobs, or you might need your manager to agree. You need to be clear about what you want and where you want to go. And you have to let your manager know this and get the development and training you need to meet the criteria.

I once heard a woman speak at a conference. She was CEO of a bank in New York. She had always wanted that job but kept being offered other positions. Eventually she refused one of these positions and said which job she really wanted. Her manager said he had no idea she was even remotely interested in that job which involved an overseas relocation. 18 months later the position became vacant and she was offered the job. Now of course she had all the pre-requisite skills and experience but the important thing is that she had set her own goal and then she let people know. Many of us set goals for ourselves but it is incredibly important to let people senior to us know what these goals are. If we take the attitude, 'Well the organisation knows best; I'll see what they have in mind for me' you could miss out on your dream job. Don't give away your power to other people and leave them to decide your fate. Be pro-active – it's your career and it's your life.

Self-Reflection 9

Did you ever lose out on an opportunity because you weren't willing to go for your goal? Have you set important goals for yourself? Have you let your manager know what your goals are? Can you think where you paid the price for leaving your career plans in the hands of your organisation or company?

Removing this barrier

- Have a conversation with your manager this week about the next job you want
- Let three other people in your network know about your career plans
- Consider signing up for a course or another degree to enhance your career prospects

Barrier 10 – *'I want to be liked.'*

In spite of all the progress women have made there are still many women who, from babyhood, are encouraged to be quiet, be nice, be pretty. We get our rewards from pleasing other people. This means that much of our self-assessment is about how much approval we get from others. Of course it feels good to be liked, but this conditioning leads us to evaluate actions we should take based on what the approval rating is going to be instead of what is best for us.

As we are growing up we maybe switch our point of reference from our family to our friends so we want their approval and risk the wrath of our parents. But our internal motivation is the same – to be liked. The reality, of course, is that we can't please all of the people all of the time. But because we are desperate to be liked, if we are not liked we take it very personally – there must be something wrong with me – and our self-esteem takes a huge hit.

Now if we are coming from a perspective of wanting to be liked at work, and taking it personally if we aren't, then this is the kind of thing that might be happening:

Mary came into work one morning and bumped into a colleague Jim. He spoke to her but she ignored him. He turned to his colleague and said, 'Don't know what's up with Mary. She got out of bed the wrong side today. I'll keep out of her way today.'

Mary carried on down the corridor and bumped into Jean who also spoke to her and whom Mary also ignored. Jean turned to her colleague and said, 'Oh my, I must have upset Mary – has she said anything to you? I mean she was OK yesterday when I spoke with her. There must have been something I've done. Do you think I should go and see her?'

If Jean wants to go to see Mary because she genuinely wants to see if there is anything that is upsetting Mary that she can help with then that's fine. But if she is going to see Mary to find out what has happened and reassure herself that Mary still likes her then that is not fine. How interesting that the guy just saw Mary's behaviour as Mary's problem but Jean saw it as Jean's problem.

It is because we are running on a platform of "I want to be liked" that we find it hard to refuse requests. We fear that if we say no we won't be liked. In the workplace we must not let our "I want to be liked" platform take precedence over our competency platform. Many women find it very hard to get the balance right. We are either driven by our need to be liked, sometimes to the detriment of our performance, or we are so set on our performance that we distance ourselves from everyone and project an image of coldness and harshness. It might take us a while to weave our way through this. If you are a manager or leader, your wanting to be liked by everyone at all times can result in failure to make unpopular decisions, failure to issue instructions, failure to refuse unreasonable requests and so on. It's unrealistic to think that everyone should like everyone else. I'm sure you don't like everyone you meet. Just because someone doesn't like you doesn't mean you are not doing a good job. If your driving force is to be liked it will impair your ability to be a leader.

When I was a young schoolteacher I overheard two of my teenage pupils talking about me. One said, 'I hate her,' and the other said, 'Yes, but she's a really good teacher.' I found it hard because I wanted to be a good teacher *and* be liked. But sometimes we will be in work situations where that isn't possible. Who knows why that pupil didn't like me? The reality is that, try as we might, we can never make people like us. We have absolutely no control over what someone else thinks of us.

So better to constantly review our performance: am I being fair, competent, efficient, caring? And, in addition, work on our need to be liked.

Self-Reflection 10

How comfortable are you with being disliked? Do you make efforts to make sure that people like you? Do you take it personally if people don't like you?

Removing this barrier

- Write down 10 things you like about yourself and read that list last thing at night and first thing in the morning
- Spend time with people who think you're great
- Smile when you hear or sense that someone doesn't like you, and like yourself more to compensate

Chapter 5

Managing the Work/Life Integration More Effectively

We all know the importance of managing home and work effectively but maybe it's more than an organisation issue. Maybe it's as much to do with organising our *thinking*. How much better would our lives be if we were to stop feeling guilty so much of the time and learned how to say no?

In this chapter:

▶ Our double bind

▶ Dealing with the guilt trip

▶ The key to it all: being able to say no to requests

▶ Tried and tested time tips

Our double bind

I'd like to share a poem with you by Natasha Josefowitz from her book *Is This Where I was Going?*

The New Double Binds

We're damned if we do and damned if we don't.
I'm either screwing up or being screwed.
If I'm home with the kids, I'm not liberated.
If I go to work, I'm a bad mother.
I either don't do enough for my husband (according to his mother),
or I do too much (according to mine).
If I'm too pretty, I won't get hired because I'll distract the men.
If I'm too plain, I won't get hired. Who wants unattractive females around?
If I wear my 3-piece suit, I look too mannish.
If I wear a dress, I'm not professional.
If I bring in the coffee, that's all I'm good for.
If I don't, I'm one of those women's libbers.
If I eat lunch with my boss, the secretaries gossip.
If I eat with the secretaries, I'm seen as just one of the girls.
If I don't work overtime, women want special consideration.
If I do, I'm a rate buster.
If I ask her to retype a letter, women bosses are bitches.
If I don't, I have no standards.
If I agree, I have no opinions.
If I disagree, I'm aggressive.
If I smile, I'm seductive.
If I don't, I'm cold.
If I stop this list here, I haven't said enough, and if I don't, it will get too long.
So damned if we don't and still, damned if we do.
I'll just be like me and you be like you.

So here's the thing? How do we be like us? What are we like, actually? And how can we be true to ourselves while managing all the various aspects of our lives – the juggle and the struggle as I call it.

We already looked at how we can be split between the feminine and masculine sides of ourselves in Chapter 2. In this chapter, we're going to look at the tension between the two predominant roles of women – that of the worker, and that of the mother/sister/carer/volunteer. Not all women are mothers of course, but it is likely that, unless you are living on your own, you probably have more than your share of the responsibility in managing the home where you live.

Dealing with the guilt trip

Let's begin by looking at this issue of guilt. We feel guilty when we don't do something we think we should have done or when we do something we think we shouldn't have done. I want to share a story with you about something that happened to me 25 years ago.

My father had been taken into hospital with a lung infection. He had a history of heart problems but this infection was nothing to do with his heart. He had been in hospital for four days and I was in close touch with my brother who lived nearby. I lived two and a half hours drive away. On the evening of the fourth day I asked my brother to ask the doctor if it was serious and if I should come. He phoned me back at 10pm when he got home (no mobile phones in those days). The doctor had said that everything was fine; there was no cause for alarm and no need for the family to come.

As I sat on the side of my bed at 11pm that night I thought about whether or not I should go. The doctor said not to and if I did go how long would I stay? Until he came out of hospital? After that even? It was impossible to tell how quickly he would get better and at this stage I had no reason to think he wouldn't.

So here is the question I asked myself: 'If you go to bed now and your dad dies tonight will you be able to live with yourself?' I knew that if the answer was 'No I wouldn't, I would be guilty forever' then I had no option but to get in the car and drive to him. But in the light of all the evidence and the medical advice I decided that in the event that my father *did* die, that I *could* live with myself. That this was the best decision I could make – for tonight at least.

I got the phone call from my brother at about 2:45am saying I should come straight away. I dressed hurriedly and left leaving my husband behind with the children. Apparently my brother phoned again at 3:15am saying there was no point – I was too late. But of course there was no way to contact me so on I drove to the hospital getting there at about 5:30am. I knew as soon as I arrived at the hospital and they took me into a small room that I was too late. Everyone had already gone home with my mother. I am still so thankful that there were no mobile phones because if there had been I may well have driven straight to my mother's. As it was, I had a precious hour alone with my father to say goodbye. His spirit was still there. I could feel his presence in the room. He had waited for me.

And was I guilty? No I wasn't. Why? Because I had made a conscious decision to not go, knowing there was a slight chance that something could happen. Part of decision-making is living with the consequences. There is no greater responsibility than accepting the consequences of the decisions we make.

And I learnt something important about guilt. We cannot live in the world of "should" and "ought" and "supposed to". Those words signify that we really don't want to but if we don't we'll feel really guilty. So next time you feel a "should" coming on ask yourself: what will be the consequence if I *don't* do this and can I live with that? If you decide that you wouldn't be able to live with the consequences then go ahead and do whatever it is. But know that now you are doing it from a place of want, not ought, so you can do it with graciousness. And if you choose not to do it you are already prepared to face the consequences for you have chosen them. Now your courage will see you through.

So my tip for you is to start developing courage and practising graciousness. And leaving guilt outside the door where it belongs.

Self-Reflection 1

Are there things you feel guilty about? List them all and say which is at the top of your list, i.e. the thing you feel *most* guilty about or the thing you feel guilty about *a lot* of the time. Now look at what you can put in place to reduce your guilt. What thinking do you need to change?

The key to it all: being able to say no to requests

Now let's move onto the issue of saying no to requests, and in particular saying no without feeling guilty. Listen to this scenario:

It's the end of a long day. You've been overloaded with work by a manager who gives you other people's tasks as well as your own because you are so very competent. On your way home you meet a neighbour. You agree to do her a "small favour" by looking after her children at the weekend as well as your own. You arrive home late and are greeted in the hall by your children who want to know if you can drive them round to a friend's house. Your daughter wants to know if she can borrow a scarf you haven't even worn yet. In the midst of all this your mother rings up and wants to chat about the awful day she's had. On his way out, your partner asks if you fancy going bowling at the weekend with some mutual friends. You hate bowling! An hour later, when you are just beginning to unwind, a friend rings you to ask if she can "call round for an hour" – just when you thought you had the evening to yourself. Sound familiar?

Self-Reflection 2

Do you have a problem refusing things you don't want to do? What things do you find it hard to say no to?

A lot of women find it very hard to refuse requests and invitations, especially when they come in the form of interruptions. If you are pressed for time, then it's a frequent but foolish response to agree to something just in order to get rid of the other person because you and I know we will certainly repent at leisure. You can't do everything you are asked and you have to accept this. Not all requests are reasonable and then there are some that are simply undesirable. Yet people often believe that they don't have the right to refuse and they agree in order to please – and then of course, they feel annoyed later for having done so.

Actually, refusing requests is one of our basic rights. But women in particular find this difficult. This is partly because we've been brought up to put other people's needs first, but also because we worry about the impact that a refusal will have on other people and our relationship with them – will they be angry? It's a difficult reaction to cope with for many women. Therefore, what do we do? We agree and end up doing what we don't want to do.

How many times do you find yourself saying yes when you really want to say no? Think back to the time when you agreed to do something which you were reluctant to do, not things you *want* to do or which you are happy to do to help someone out. I'm talking about the things you do because you can't refuse. Sometimes we are taken off guard by a request and we don't have time to consider it properly so we say yes because we don't like to offend. Here are the things we might feel when this happens:

- Resentful towards the other person for asking
- Annoyed with ourselves for accepting
- Frustrated at the misuse of our time

So why do we do it then? Here are some reasons:

- We believe it's selfish or uncaring to refuse
- Other people expect us to agree
- The person making the request will be angry or hurt if we refuse
- We think it's impolite to refuse
- We'd feel guilty if we refused
- We're afraid we wouldn't be liked if we refused

Self-Reflection 3

Why do you think you agree to do things you don't want to do?

Here are some golden rules to help us to decide whether to say no.

1. Your time is as valuable as someone else's, and this includes your partner, your children, your relatives and your friends.
2. You have the right to refuse some requests that are made of you – and the responsibility to accept the consequences.

3. When you say no you are refusing the request and not rejecting the person.

This last one is *so* important. And we need to remember that when we get refused something too.

Learning to say no is a skill, which is good news because skills can be learned and improved with practice. (If you have read my book *Reclaim Your Power, Reclaim Your Life*, you will remember that saying no is also covered in that book. But because it is so important to learn how to say no, I am including in in this book too!)

We are going to look at this in some detail because it is hard for many women – especially if they have a "*like me*" block. Here are the steps involved.

1. Assess the request.

Ask yourself, 'Do I really want to do this?' The very fact that you have to ask this question may indicate that you are not happy to accept. Pausing, even for a moment, will give you an opportunity to consider your response.

Then assess:

- Is this a reasonable request?
- Is it a priority?
- Do I want to do it?
- What are the consequences of refusing?
- Can I live with the consequences?

Now, it's hard to assess all this on the spot, so the next thing you need to do is...

2. Buy some time.

Whatever someone asks you to do, you do not have to answer immediately. You might want to explore the issues. You might want to explore how urgent is it and does it have to be done by you anyway? You can be concerned about their situation, but you don't need to give into their request immediately. So don't respond straight away but assess the request and, if necessary, ask for more information or clarification.

For instance, you can say:

- *Let me think about that.*
- *I can't give you an answer right now.*

- *Can I come back to you on that?*

It's no bad thing to practise, so whatever someone asks you to do always say: 'Let me think about that and I will get back to you.' Whether you'll get back to them in 10 minutes or tomorrow, get in the habit of buying yourself some time. It allows you to think about whether you want to accept or refuse, and how you will refuse if you do.

3. Use an alternative to the word no.

It can sound harsh to simply say no to somebody:

'Can you give me a lift into town tonight after work?'
'No.'

And it might sound downright rude sometimes. There are other ways.

You could say:

- *I don't want to*
- *I prefer not to*
- *I'd rather not*
- *I'm not happy to*
- *It's not possible*

There are plenty of alternatives that can be used instead of the word no. Get used to using them.

4. Don't apologise if you don't mean it.

Many women apologise profusely often. They begin a refusal with, 'I'm awfully sorry, but...' No. Apologise only if you are genuinely sorry that you can't do what someone has asked and then your apology will be sincere.

Here is an example:

'Can you give me a lift into town?'
'Oh, I'm sorry, I can't. I'm not going into town tonight, I have to pick John up.'

Now, if you are genuinely sorry that you can't help, apologising is a way of expressing this. If you are not sorry, then a better response would be, 'It's not possible tonight. I have to pick John up.' And if you actually want to express regret but want to get out of the habit of saying the word sorry, you can say, 'It's not possible tonight. I have to pick John up. Otherwise I would be glad to.'

It's a good idea to adopt this way of expressing regret in preference to saying the word sorry. Try and cut that word out altogether for a while. If you do you'll realise just how often you want to say it!

5. Don't make excuses, but give honest reasons if you wish.

Never refuse a request by saying, 'I can't because...' because as soon as you give a reason it invites someone to sort out the reason why you can't do it and take away your excuse. And once you have no excuse you have to do it. So saying 'I can't because' as an excuse is not a very tactical thing to do.

What's more, if it sounds like an excuse it also sounds like you accept that you really ought to agree. So don't invite someone to solve the problem why you can't do it as you'll be left with nowhere to go.

You can give a simple reason and then it sounds less abrupt than a straight no:

'Shall we go for a walk?'
'I don't want to. It's too cold.'

'Can you stay late tomorrow?'
'Unfortunately not – I have an engagement after work.'

If you want to, of course, give honest reasons but that is not the same as making excuses.

6. Explain the consequences or look at the possibilities.

You could say:

- *I could do it tomorrow instead.*
- *Which of my other tasks shall I leave to get this one done?*
- *If I do this, I won't get the figures complete for the meeting on Monday.*

Explaining the consequences to the person can help the person rethink the request they made of you. Remember to speak slowly and steadily: you have a right to refuse the request. As we covered earlier, refusing the request is not rejecting the person: it's just refusing the request. You might feel that at work you are in no position to refuse but you can certainly point out the consequences of what they are asking as in the bullet points above.

7. Watch your body language.

We are going to be looking at this in Chapter 7 in relation to making presentations, but body language is important no matter what the situation.

Your face, body and movements should always reinforce what you are saying. So take care with the following:

- If you smile, it contradicts and undermines what you are saying
- If your voice is harsh or abrupt you may offend
- If your voice is low and you look apologetic it may encourage the other person to try and persuade you
- If you fidget or appear nervous it may seem that you don't really mean what you are saying

Speak slowly and calmly and maintain eye contact, make your movements natural and match your facial expression with your words. Once you can master the art of saying no you'll find the payoffs to be immense:

- You won't feel the need to lie
- You won't agree to an unwelcome request then have to wriggle out of it
- You are less likely to feel guilty
- You will communicate better with people
- You will be respected for your honesty – people can see through excuses
- You will have more time for *your* priorities
- You will have more control over your life

Self-Reflection 4

What are you going to try to put into practice this month
when it comes to refusing requests?

Tried and tested time tips

Finally, let's look at some tried and tested time tips. If you can afford to have paid help for washing, ironing, cooking, childcare, then some of the following tips might not be relevant for you. And I'm sure that you are already doing many of these things – we have to, (right?), in order to survive! But hopefully there will be something here for everyone. We're going to look at seven ways in which you can save time and five things to remember as you manage your work/life integration.

1. Plan meals.

Planning meals in advance means you can get the ingredients from the supermarket when you go to do a bulk shop instead of at the expensive local shop at the last minute. I'm actually in favour of supporting local enterprises instead of global chains but I'm also in favour of helping women to save time. Planning can also include who does the cooking. When my eldest daughter was 13 we also had an 18-year-old living with us and they each cooked twice a week. They decided what to cook, which days they would cook and it was up to them to make sure the ingredients went on the shopping list for the Friday evening shop. And as Friday night was takeaway night it meant that I didn't have to think about food and cooking during the week – bliss!

2. Use a master shopping list.

The shopping was done weekly and my then-husband and I would take the list and would do the shop. But the problem for me was that I was the one who did the list. I wrote out what we needed and did it or I gave it to my husband and he did it. I realised I needed to lessen my load and make everyone responsible, not just me.

What I did took some time, but it was worth it. I created a master list of everything that we needed in the cupboards at any one time and divided it into areas. Whoever was responsible for doing that part of the list (e.g. tinned goods) would look in the cupboard, see there was only one tin of chopped tomatoes, check the master list, which would say there should be four, and therefore know to write three tins of chopped tomatoes on the weekly list.

What happened very quickly was they started to do for their area what I was able to do: open the cupboard, quickly look in and see what was missing, and write it down.

When we were all doing it, it didn't take very long for everyone to do their section and, although it meant the shopping list was done in different handwritings, who cared? I was only doing a fraction of what I used to do and *everyone* was taking some responsibility.

3. Cook in bulk.

And before we leave the issue of food entirely it's worth mentioning cooking in bulk. I don't mean cooking a week's meals in one go – although some people do this – I mean cooking double or even triple of a meal you are preparing anyway. Freeze the rest in individual portions and you have some great ready-made home-cooked meals for those days when you arrive home late and are just too tired to get yourself something to eat.

4. Buy in bulk.

This works for food of course but it also works for other things – especially those items you never have around when you need them like tights, birthday cards, wrapping paper and stamps. I also got tired of rushing out to buy last minute birthday presents because one of my children was going to a birthday party and didn't have a present to take. So whenever I was out and saw bargain gifts for children I would buy a couple and put them in the "present box" then when there was a party to go to, one of the girls could go to the present box and choose a suitable gift. This also works for my female friends. I always like to take a little gift if I go to stay somewhere so I collect small inexpensive items and keep them in my present drawer so I always have a little something for a friend when I need it.

5. Use lists.

I've mentioned a master shopping list but how about a wall calendar in the kitchen which can be used for all the family activities – football, dancing, visiting Gran, days out. One list I created was a meal planner headed with days, person cooking, meal planned, people eating, special notes. This is useful for the cooks as they need to know how many to cook for. And if friends are coming back for tea they need to be added to the list. Another list can make the taxi service we run for our children a little easier to manage. Make sure they put on the list dates, places and times so you can plan your time or arrange their transport. And do encourage your children to do their own lists too. It's possible for them to start to take responsibility especially when it comes to remembering things for school (we'll look at delegating responsibility in a moment). And the best thing about lists is that once something has been written down then you can forget what it was you were trying to remember.

6. Prepare the night before.

Once my youngest daughter had started school we used to have a routine on a Saturday morning with her older sister because they each took sandwiches for their lunch. They would choose from the supermarket what they wanted on their sandwiches, then we'd have a little setup on the kitchen table where they would butter the bread, make the sandwiches, cut them into four, put them in polythene bags, and put them in the freezer. Then every day, as they went out to school, they would take a bag out of the freezer, which would be thawed by the time it got to lunchtime. So they were being responsible for (a) choosing what went on their sandwiches, (b) making them and (c) getting them out of the freezer in the morning. Wonderful!

When my older daughter was about 10 she told me she was having lunch with her friends when one said, 'I wonder what I've got on my sandwiches today.' Lucy said, 'What do you mean? Don't you make them yourself?' She replied, 'No, my mum does.' Lucy asked her, 'Does your mother work outside of the home?' and her friend said, 'Yes.' Then Lucy said, 'So she has a job outside of the home and she's working in the house and she has to make your sandwiches as well for lunch when you could make them yourself and decide what goes on them? That's ridiculous.' And all her friends agreed, so much so that they all started making their own sandwiches for lunch. I often wondered if those mothers realised they owed me a debt of gratitude for that!

7. Delegate responsibility.

Why do parents have to remember that today the school photographer is coming or that they need to take their wellington boots for the nature trip or that they need to take their scrap book in to school? Children can learn very quickly that they are responsible for their own destiny – it's in their interests to get themselves organised. You don't do them any favours by doing all their thinking for them. If my daughters came home from school and said, 'We need to take money for the school photograph on Friday,' or 'We're going on a field trip on Thursday and will need our boots.' I would say, 'OK. Well you need to make sure you remember then. Write it on a sticky note and put it over your bed or on your bedroom door so you don't forget.' They realised very quickly it was up to them to remember it. I would say to them: 'Look, if you forget your boots for the field trip, you will miss the field trip. You are the ones who need to remember it.' It makes them into very responsible people.

Self-Reflection 5

Which of these ways to save time do you think you could start to do?
What others can you think of?

Finally, here are the five things to remember as you integrate home and work, and work and the rest of your life.

1. Don't try to be perfect – superwoman is a fictional character.
2. Don't waste time worrying – it's a useless emotion.
3. Keep your sense of humour – not difficult if you have children.
4. Be flexible. Try things out and if they don't work, try something else.
5. Ask for what you need. Your needs are equally as important as everyone else's. Never forget that.

Self-Reflection 6

What would you do with the extra time if you could create some?
And what will you do to make sure you do?

Chapter 6

Thriving Not Surviving

How vulnerable are you to stress? And how do you react to stress?
It's important to identify what causes you stress, and what you
can do about it so you can be hardy, healthy and happy.

In this chapter:

- ▶ Checking your vulnerability and reactions to stress
- ▶ Short-term strategies that work, and ones that don't
- ▶ The REACH strategy for managing stress
- ▶ The REACH strategy in practice
- ▶ 10 quick tips for thriving not surviving
- ▶ Ways to deal with potential stressors
- ▶ Hardy, Healthy, Happy action plan

Checking your vulnerability and reactions to stress

The higher up the ladder you go the more imperative it is that you can handle the big job, your family and yourself without any one of them collapsing. So being more aware of your **own** stress triggers *and* having a strategy to deal with stress will become increasingly important.

Let's be clear about the difference between pressure and stress. Pressure is not intrinsically harmful. Pressure can provide challenge and stimulus, enabling people to mobilise their resources to get things done. But when pressure affects us adversely then it becomes stress. Being aware of the causes, the effects and having a variety of ways to control the pressure in your life is 90% of the solution. So this chapter is about increasing your awareness of all these things so that you can move from surviving to thriving. As we work through this topic there are a couple of questionnaires to do and space for you to start an action plan at the end. So instead of the usual Self-Reflection questions I invite you to set aside an hour to read, do the work, reflect and come up with your own action plan.

So let's start with the causes of stress.

We are all familiar with what I call the usual stressors based on events:

- Death of a child, partner, family member or close friend
- Divorce or separation
- Getting married
- Pregnancy
- Starting a new job
- Christmas
- Taking on a mortgage

It's interesting that something that we might choose, like getting married or a new job, is still capable of causing us much stress.

For many people, our job is a huge cause of stress in itself, which might be related to the nature of the job; the culture of the organisation; career development or lack of it; and unclear roles and relationships at work especially with our manager.

Whatever stress men have at work – there is additional stress for women. Here are four reasons why:

1. They are subjected to double standards: women are pushy or bossy, whereas men are leaders and decisive.
2. They have few role models to follow and those who have achieved promotion are often isolated and unsure of themselves.
3. Some women have difficulty being assertive and lack confidence.
4. They often have multiple roles and responsibilities because of their home/ work situation.

Add to that issues to do with male bosses (like 'my male boss feels threatened by me' and 'I have to work harder than anyone else to prove myself); issues to do with female bosses (like 'my female boss is very intimidating' and 'my female boss doesn't give me extra help because *she* didn't get any); and issues to do with male colleagues (as in 'my male colleagues exclude me from what is going on' and 'my male colleagues do not take me seriously'). And on top of all *that* we have to deal with the wonder woman syndrome and the lack of support.

So what are the issues you face daily as a working woman, and maybe a working mother, that cause you to feel stressed and guilty?

Look at this list and tick the statements that seem to be true for you. We'll be looking at how you can deal with all these stressors later in the chapter.

Potential Stressors

☐ *I meet few women in positions similar to mine.*

☐ *I am too tired to cope with my family's needs.*

☐ *I can't relax at home because there is too much to do.*

☐ *I am expected to take work home.*

☐ *I have most of the responsibility for running the home.*

☐ *I feel guilty if I am late home.*

☐ *I have to prove to myself that I am a super partner/mother/manager.*

☐ *I have to prove to others that I am a super mother/partner/manager.*

☐ *I work extra hard at being a good mother/partner to make up for the time I'm at work.*

☐ *I have no/hardly any time to myself.*

- ☐ *I feel people are waiting for me to say that I can't cope.*
- ☐ *If the house doesn't run perfectly I get the blame.*
- ☐ *If the house doesn't run perfectly I accept the blame.*
- ☐ *My family don't take my work seriously.*
- ☐ *My friends don't want to talk about my work.*
- ☐ *My family would prefer me not to work.*
- ☐ *I'm always justifying that the family isn't suffering because I work.*

I wonder how many men worry about these things? Maybe you only have a couple of ticks, which is great news! We'll come back later and look at what you can do about them.

But first we need to examine how vulnerable you are to stress, and how you react to stress.

Let's start by looking at your vulnerability. Look at each of the questions in the following exercise and score each question 3, 1 or 0. A score of 3 means you can definitely say **Yes** to the statement and think the statement is absolutely true for you.

Example 1: *I spend time walking each day.* If you do walk every day then score 3; if you walk some days score 1 and if you never have a walk score 0.

Example 2: *I avoid drinking at lunchtimes.* If that is true and you *never* drink at lunchtimes then score 3; if you occasionally drink at lunchtimes score 1 and if you drink nearly every lunchtime score 0.

Complete the exercise now. There are 48 questions but it will only take you a few moments to complete it. Write your scores next to each question as you go along and when you have finished transfer them to the table on the following page. Or, add them directly to the table as you go if you prefer.

How vulnerable am I to stress?

1. I eat the right food in the right quantities.
2. I avoid drinking alcohol at lunchtimes.
3. I exercise to the point of perspiration at least three times a week.
4. I have a network of friends and acquaintances.
5. I am contented with my sex life.

6. I have at least one hobby/interest I pursue regularly.
7. I never work at weekends.
8. I engage regularly in prayer or meditation.
9. I limit my intake of coffee, tea and fizzy drinks to five cups a day.
10. I enjoy a drink of alcohol rather than **needing** a drink, or I do not drink alcohol.
11. I exert moderate physical energy in my daily life.
12. I give and receive affection regularly.
13. I regularly achieve sexual satisfaction.
14. I allow myself time to relax every day.
15. I restrict myself to realistic workloads and never work to excess.
16. I usually find solutions to my problems.
17. I maintain the appropriate weight for my height.
18. I never drink alcohol alone.
19. I climb the stairs rather than use the lift.
20. I am able to show emotions rather than allow negative feelings to build up inside me.
21. I am seldom unable or not wanting to have sex.
22. I get 7-8 hours sleep at least four nights a week.
23. I never let work dominate my life.
24. I believe in myself.
25. I avoid adding too much salt to my food.
26. I rarely have a drink of alcohol when I get home from work.
27. I follow a regular programme of exercise.
28. I have people who are close to me with whom I can discuss intimate problems.
29. I have a loving sexual relationship.
30. I do something for fun at least once a week.
31. I avoid talking about work in social situations.
32. I have an inner feeling of tranquility.
33. I eat regular meals each day and avoid frequent snacks.
34. I would describe myself as a moderate drinker of alcohol (an average of one drink per day) or I do not drink alcohol at all.
35. I participate in a sport each week.
36. I have colleagues at work who give me emotional support.
37. I am in a stable intimate relationship.
38. I am able to enjoy myself.

39. I never work in the evenings.
40. I feel I have a deep sense of belonging, of being a part of things.
41. I drink water/mineral water regularly.
42. I do not smoke at all.
43. I spend time walking each day.
44. I would seek help from friends or obtain professional advice if necessary.
45. I seldom feel sexually frustrated.
46. I am able to spend time doing nothing.
47. My home life and work is equally important to me.
48. I have learnt to rise above stressful situations.

Once you've filled in the chart, add up the numbers in each of the columns to get a total score for each letter.

	A		B		C		D		E		F		G		H
Q1		Q2		Q3		Q4		Q5		Q6		Q7		Q8	
Q 9		Q10		Q11		Q12		Q13		Q14		Q15		Q16	
Q 17		Q18		Q19		Q20		Q21		Q22		Q23		Q24	
Q 25		Q26		Q27		Q28		Q29		Q30		Q31		Q32	
Q 33		Q34		Q35		Q36		Q37		Q38		Q39		Q40	
Q 41		Q42		Q43		Q44		Q45		Q46		Q47		Q48	
Total															

A = Healthy diet
B = Avoiding alcohol and cigarettes
C = Exercise
D = Emotional wellbeing
E = Fulfilling sex life
F = Relaxation and enjoyment
G = Balance between home and work
H = Self-understanding and acceptance

Look at your scores for each area. The higher your score the less vulnerable you are to stress:

- 13-18 indicates that in this area you have a strong barrier and defence against stress.
- 7-12 indicates that you have some resistance to stress but not very much if

you are under a great deal of it.

- 0-6 indicates that you have a very high vulnerability to stress.

Now you need to examine these areas. Do you think they are a fair reflection of your stress vulnerability? A questionnaire is a tool to develop self-awareness (a key leadership skill remember?) and by now you should have enough understanding of yourself to decide whether the results are a true reflection or not.

One woman who did this exercise said: 'I know that I should have a healthy diet, exercise and avoid alcohol and cigarettes. But I liked this exercise because for the first time I saw some positive scores in my stress management. It did me good to realise that my ability to give and receive affection and my ability to have fun and relax are positive stress management strategies. It's given me the impetus to improve in the other areas.'

Look at the areas where you seem to be the most vulnerable (where you had the lowest scores) and read the questions as suggestions for what you can immediately put in place to increase your defences against stress.

Here is what to do to reduce your vulnerability to stress:

- Look at which area you want to improve and add this to your Hardy, Healthy, Happy action plan (at the end of this chapter) and write down what you're going to do to improve this column score
- Where you scored a 0 or 1, choose which five you will address straight away
- Make a 3-month action plan and choose some different things each week and each month to work on

Making some of these changes is a long-term job. It's not going to happen overnight but it's imperative that you put some things in place now to protect yourself from the increasing pressures you are going to face in your leadership career.

Now we need to look at how you usually react to stress. There's another questionnaire for you to do. If the statement applies to you at present, or has applied to you in the last 12 months, or at a time when you were experiencing intense stress then tick it. Be as honest as you can when you respond to each statement – no one is going to see this only you. Add your ticks to the score chart on the following page, but pay attention to how the boxes are numbered; it isn't chronological.

What are my usual reactions to stress?

1. I am easily irritated.
2. I have difficulty concentrating for any length of time.
3. I feel tired even when I wake up in the morning.
4. I seem to have boundless energy.
5. I cannot make fairly trivial decisions.
6. I have difficulty getting to sleep and/or I wake during the night and am restless.
7. I am achieving far more work than usual.
8. I am losing my temper very frequently.
9. I feel generally run down and rather unwell.
10. I am able to concentrate fully on what I am doing.
11. Life seems to be quite hopeless. Nothing seems worthwhile and I feel really low.
12. I have lost my appetite or I seem to be eating more food to comfort myself.
13. I have difficulty in absorbing new data.
14. I suffer from frequent headaches.
15. I am able to respond quickly to the demands placed upon me.
16. I have difficulty recalling information when I am required to do so.
17. I am drinking more alcohol than usual.
18. I experience dramatic mood swimgs: sometimes I feel quite elated; at other times I feel very depressed.
19. I often feel exhilarated about what I am doing.
20. I have missed, or been late for, one or two important appointments.
21. I feel wound up and am unable to relax properly.
22. I am unable to achieve my normal level of creativity.
23. I suffer from backache regularly.
24. Ideas seem to flow more easily than usual.
25. I feel tearful if criticised.
26. I have taken time off work.
27. I suffer frequently from indigestion.
28. I seem to lack the capacity to focus on a particular problem – my mind keeps wandering to other issues.
29. Little things send me into panic. I feel as if I am unable to cope.
30. I have been smoking more cigarettes than usual.
31. I have a frequent need to urinate.
32. In discussion with other people I constantly repeat myself.

33. My driving is rather erratic and my judgement impaired.
34. I seem to worry about many things.
35. I am mentally and/or physically very active.

	A		B		C		D		E
Q1		Q2		Q3		Q6		Q4	
Q8		Q5		Q9		Q12		Q7	
Q11		Q13		Q14		Q17		Q10	
Q18		Q16		Q21		Q20		Q15	
Q25		Q22		Q23		Q26		Q19	
Q29		Q28		Q27		Q30		Q24	
Q34		Q32		Q31		Q33		Q35	
Total									

A = Emotional reactions

B = Disruptions of thought processes

C = Physical illnesses

D = Behavioural indicators

E = Positive reactions

Add up the amount of ticks you have in each area:

- 5-7 in any column indicates a very strong reaction – unhelpful in every category except Category E.
- 2-4 indicates a manageable reaction
- 0-1 indicates this isn't an issue for you

Again, look at whether you think this is true for you. Where does your stress show? Emotionally? In your behaviour? In illness? And what are the costs of these reactions? Give yourself credit for where you have scored in the statements for positive reactions (4, 7, 10, 15, 19, 25 and 35). The more we can have these statements be true for us the more we will be thriving not surviving! And for the areas you want to improve in, make a note on your Hardy, Healthy and Happy action plan.

I wonder from your experience and observation whether you think that men and women react differently to stress? It's a commonly held theory that women have high emotional reactions to stress and men have high disruption of thought patterns. Do you think this is true? I think that women may be judged more harshly if they have an emotional reaction to stress than men whose thinking becomes clouded – even though they may both be reacting to the same amount of stress. What do you think?

The good news is that we can change these reactions to stress. We've already looked at how we can limit how vulnerable we are to stress in the first place. Now it's time to look at what we can do to deal with the stress we **do** have to face in our lives, without paying the price in terms of illness or emotional reaction or any of the other negative ways.

Short-term strategies that work, and ones that don't

There are six short-term strategies we can use to deal with stress. Three are good and three are to be avoided.

Let's take a look at the ones to be avoided first.

Denial

- Getting depressed because you think you should cope but deep down knowing that you're not doing
- Erratic behavior – sometimes high; sometimes low
- Putting a brick wall up and appearing very defensive

Sometimes people refuse to accept they are under stress because they can't face the reality of having to do something about it. Denying that the problem exists may be a desperate attempt to drive it away, but failing to tackle it just makes the problem worse. If you refuse to acknowledge that there is a problem you also repress the feelings that are associated with it. The fact that expressing your feelings is often socially unacceptable makes the situation worse for someone in a management or leadership position, particularly if the manager is female and therefore automatically labelled emotional, neurotic and not cut out for the job. If you scored high in the "emotional reactions" in the last exercise might it be that you are trying to deny that you are stressed at all and soldier on regardless? It's not good to repress feelings: it can lead to depression and physical illness. So it's very important that we don't deny that we are under stress when we clearly are.

Escape

- Over indulging – smoking, drinking more than usual
- Throwing energy into areas which are not related to the one which is the problem

Smoking, drugs and alcohol are three examples of this kind of temporary relief, which many people resort to when they are under stress. Of course, all of these can easily lead to other problems, which aggravate the original source of stress. It's good to relax with a drink after a hard day at work – but if you find you are turning to drink or you *need* a drink so you can forget about the stress you are under then this "escape and forget" strategy doesn't really help in the long run.

Displacement

- Taking it out on others – at work and at home
- Short-tempered with others
- Critical
- Unreasonable

This occurs when people who are suffering from stress cause others to feel stressed too. Their efforts to cope are at the expense of those around them. Instead of confronting and tackling the source of stress, they redirect it to those they are working or living with and become short-tempered, critical and unreasonable. This method of coping has disastrous implications for the organisation they work for and can seriously affect the performance of the whole team.

Now let's look at some short-term strategies which *do* work.

Distraction

- Exercise
- Having a massage/facial
- Cooking/baking
- Walking the dog
- Doing something new or creative

Distraction means acknowledging that the problem exists but taking yourself away from it just for a while in order to restore your peace of mind. It's a form of temporary relief, which can improve your capacity to tackle the problem by restoring your mental and physical fitness.

Emotional release

- Crying
- Laughing
- Thumping a pillow
- Writing a diary
- Phoning a friend
- Dancing

- Singing

This means letting off steam in some way by channelling frustrations, pent up feelings and even rage into a harmless pursuit. If you think of yourself under stress as a pot boiling over, you can help the situation a little by draining off some of the contents of the pot. Release your emotions by doing what comes naturally.

Self-care
- Yoga
- Listening to music
- Relaxing/meditating
- Taking a short break/holiday
- Eating healthy food
- Spending time alone

This is my favourite one. You have to make yourself a priority so you can get into the right state to be able to cope. Of course it's better if your lifestyle incorporates ways of doing this over the long term but there are short-term measures you can do.

I'm sure you can think of many other ways of distracting yourself, emotional release and self-care and if you find these things helpful in relieving stress in the short term then of course carry on using them. Think of your own ways and add to your Hardy, Healthy, Happy action plan.

The REACH strategy for managing stress

So what about a strategy for managing stress in the long term? This has to be a planned process not a quick fix. First you have to accept that there *is* something you can do. The longer you go without taking action, the more likely you are to damage your health and the more difficult it will be to control the stress. I'm going to share something with you I call the REACH strategy. I've shared it with many, many women who have found it useful and I hope you will too.

REACH stands for:

Recognise and release
Evaluate
Accept
Confront
Happy

Each one of these words represents a step in the process of coping with a particular stressor. Let's look at them in more detail.

RECOGNISE the symptoms and source and **RELEASE** your feelings.

We've already done a lot of work on recognising the symptoms of your stress. So once you've acknowledged that you are stressed (and sometimes it takes the symptoms to inform us that we are stressed) then you can go on and investigate the cause. You might know the cause to start with; the stress might be inherent in a situation you are dealing with. Releasing your feelings is important even while you are deciding on your long-term strategy and solution. You want to be coming to your decisions about a solution with a clear head.

EVALUATE the options that are open to you.

Ask yourself, 'What can I do about this particular situation?' There is usually more than one way of resolving a difficult situation. You may need to get someone else's perspective on the problem, particularly if it is one that has been bothering you for some time. Don't expect another person to make the decision for you, but talking through a problem with an interested listener often helps to clarify your own thoughts. Sometimes it's only when I hear myself saying something out loud that I realise what I actually think about it.

Then assess the consequences of each of the options that are open to you. Ask yourself, 'What is the best and worse thing that could happen if I take this action?' Sometimes we don't take action because we project a terrible outcome but that can be just our fear acting as a barrier and holding us back. And sometimes you even realise that in the cold light of day the worst thing that could happen is not that bad anyway and is outweighed by the relief of taking some action.

ACCEPT

There are three options for you here:

1. Accept that there are some things in your life that you *can* change if you want to.

Is the situation causing your stress one that you can change? Perhaps there *is* a solution that you know you will have to face eventually but you keep delaying the inevitable. Remember you have the right to make decisions for yourself and the responsibility to accept the consequences of your decision.

2. Accept that there are some things in life that you *cannot* change even if you try.

You can either accept these things that you can't change or be continually upset about them. If they are truly beyond your control, like a relative dying, then your peace will come from accepting the situation. Fighting the inevitable will increase your stress so then you have a difficult situation to deal with *and* your stress about it. Hard to do I know but we have to remember that while we can't change some situations we can control our reaction to that situation. That is probably the only true power we have: the choice about how to react.

3. Accept is that there may be some things in your life that you may not *want* to change.

The consequences of making some changes may be less acceptable than keeping things as they are – despite the stress. Some people feel they can't leave their job because they have a mortgage and bills to pay. That's true so for them at this point they are choosing to stay in their job in order to pay the mortgage and they will stay until such time they can find another job *and* pay the mortgage. So if you are tempted to say, 'But I don't have a choice' make sure that it's about something you really don't have a choice about. Or accept that you *do* have a choice and you'll stay with the current situation for now and employ more short-term strategy techniques. Just realising that you are choosing and accepting the situation for now takes some of the stress away and puts you back in control. You can still minimise the effects of the stress but you may choose to defer action that would eliminate the stress altogether. Use the next step if you have decided that you *will* take action.

CONFRONT the problem.

Confronting the problem may involve changing your perception of the situation, or saying or doing something specific to relieve the stress. You have to first choose the best of the options available to you (you've already evaluated all the options remember). Secondly, write down your objectives: what do you want to achieve? Thirdly, draw up a timescale: when do you intend to start? And fourthly, communicate to other people what you intend to do.

Confronting the problem may involve you having to face and speak to the person who is causing you stress. You will have to explain your feelings and how you would like to change the situation that exists between you at present. This part is very important: what do you want to happen? Saying how you feel is only part of the story. Remember to speak in terms of 'I' rather than 'you'. The other person is less likely to feel threatened in this way and positive and direct expression is likely to have most impact.

The final step in dealing with the stress is to implement your strategy and ask yourself: Am I **HAPPY** with the outcome? If the answer is yes then good – you have found a strategy which works for you. If the answer is no then go back to REACH and use the steps again and modify or change your approach.

That's the theory, but how does it work in practice? Here are three examples.

Sunila's story

Sunila had reached the age of 30 without making any firm decision about having a family. She worked for a publishing company in a job that was very demanding in terms of time and energy. She began to feel the pressure of her advancing years and started to agonise over whether to have a child and how she was to take care of it. She did not feel she could cope with both a child and her present job, yet she enjoyed the stimulus and income that her job brought. What made the pressures all the more difficult to bear was the fact that her husband had left the final decision to her, feeling that endless discussions about it were fruitless. Furthermore, she was suffering from the disapproval of her mother, who felt that the question of what she should do was obvious – 'settle down to raise a family'. The feeling of being in limbo was reducing her effectiveness at work. Because of the stress that she was under, Sunila felt that maybe she should put off the decision until next year.

In going through the REACH strategy, Sunila realised that there were three separate decisions to be made:

1. Whether or not to have a child?
2. If the answer was yes, how to care for the child and whether to carry on in her present job?
3. If the answer was no, what career plans should she make? And how would she deal with her mother?

She had originally confused the issues by trying to decide on all three issues simultaneously. After weighing up all the options that were open to her, Sunila decided that she was more committed to her career than to the idea of having a family. She told this to her husband and he supported her decision. The next problem was to tackle her mother, whose initial reaction was one of disbelief. Sunila accepted that her mother would probably never come to terms with the decision she had made, but refused to allow herself to be manipulated by other people's expectations of her.

Dee's story

Although she was well regarded by her team and her colleagues at work, Dee felt that she did not receive the support and encouragement she needed from her line manager. He expected her to perform well and she had never let him down. There was to be some reorganisation in the company she worked for, and in preparation for these changes, everyone was to go before a panel for a performance appraisal. The thought of this gave Dee panic attacks, particularly because she realised that a number of new senior posts were in the pipeline. She had heard her manager talking about the suitability of two of her (male) colleagues for these posts, but there had been no mention of her name. She thought about looking for another job where her loyalty and good work would be appreciated…

As she began to work through the REACH strategy, Dee recognised that she has two sources of stress:

1. The forthcoming appraisal interview
2. The lack of support from her manager

She made up her mind to tackle them separately. In order to reduce her anxieties about the interview, she assessed her strengths and weaknesses, and planned how she was going to promote her skills for the post that she was seeking. Having done some preparation, she felt more at ease about her ability to cope with any questions she might be asked. Secondly, she chose her time and place carefully, and went over in her mind exactly what she was going to say to her manager. She explained to him that she did not feel he gave her the support that she deserved. His reaction was one of surprise and he said that he did not realise that she felt that way or that she was interested in promotion. He had always been satisfied with her work and was prepared to support her application for a more senior post. Although Dee felt that her manager thought she was a bit neurotic for saying what she did, she was relieved at having expressed her feelings openly, and this helped to reduce her stress. She would not be as hesitant if a similar situation arose again.

Maria's story

Maria worked as a unit head in charge of a team of five. She was responsible for her own workload and for monitoring her team. She had problems with one of the male members of her team who felt that he was better qualified to do the job than she. He ignored her instructions and did things his way. When Maria tackled him about this, she was accused of nagging. Her next tactic was to ignore his obstructiveness in the hope that it would cease. This did not seem to work either, and caused further problems with the team, who felt he was being unfairly favoured. This source of stress, on top of the others attendant on her role as unit head, was becoming more than she could bear…

As she worked through REACH, Maria realised that the stress she felt was caused partly by her inability to face the situation. She accepted that she had to improve the performance of the "problem male" and restore her credibility with the team. She confronted the situation by arranging to speak to the person who was causing her problems. She explained how she felt about his attitude and general obstructiveness and gave him the opportunity to voice any resentment he felt at her being given the promotion. Having "cleared the air" in this way, Maria then went on to spell out what she expected of him in terms of performance. Standards were set down and agreed by both of them, to be reviewed at a future date. Although the relationship between them continued to be strained, she had regained the respect of the rest of the team by tackling the problem in this way – and removed at least one source of stress at work.

These are real stories of real women. The important thing to remember about them all is that tackling your stressful situation doesn't make your life perfect – Sunila still had to deal with her mother's disapproval and Maria still had a strained relationship with her male colleague – but taking action reduced a major part of the stress they had been feeling and meant that they could function at a higher level.

So now it's time for you to try the REACH strategy. What are you ready to tackle head on?

The REACH strategy in practice

Recognise
Evaluate
Accept
Confront
Happy

What is your stressful situation that you want to deal with?

Describe it in a few sentences.

_____

_____

_____

_____

_____

_____

Recognise and Release

What symptoms of stress are you experiencing?
What are you doing to release your feelings around this?

_____

_____

_____

_____

_____

_____

Evaluate

List all your options for dealing with this, no matter how extreme. Be creative and open-minded.

1

2

3

4

5

Accept

Accept that you *can* change all or part of this situation if you are willing to take the risk and move on to Confront.

OR

Accept that you *cannot* change the situation and that you can only change how you think about the situation and how you react to it. What attitudes can you adopt to make the situation tolerable and more interesting? What support systems can you employ to help you to maintain these attitudes? What short-term or instant relief strategies can you use to help you to stay positive and enthusiastic?

Confront

What is your best option?

_____

_____

_____

_____

What are you going to do or say and to whom?

_____

_____

_____

_____

When are you going to do this?

_____

_____

When you have put your strategy into practice record the results here. It's very important to evaluate what worked and what didn't.

Were you happy with the way it worked?

_____

If your answer is No, what exactly went wrong?

_____

_____

_____

_____

_____

Go through REACH again and decide what to do next.

Don't expect to solve your problems overnight. Something that has caused you stress for a while will not necessarily disappear quickly. However, with determination and effort, you should find a way to reduce your stress, your way.

10 quick tips for thriving not surviving

I'm sure you are already doing some of these but select the ones you are going to do more of, or start doing, and add them to your Hardy, Healthy, Happy action plan.

1. Breathe diaphragmatically.

Deep breathing from the stomach, not the chest, can reduce stress and calm you down in minutes.

2. Choose your thoughts.

Reject needless worrying and choose to focus on what you want to happen in the future. Learn positive thinking techniques and practise the mental discipline of selecting them frequently on a daily basis. Practice makes perfect and energy follows focus. So talk nicely to yourself!

3. Take exercise.

Regular exercise will cleanse the body of adrenalin and keep it healthier and happier as a consequence. Find physical activities you enjoy.

4. Regular baths/massages.

Warm muscles relax in the bath and a good shoulder and neck massage works wonders.

5. Choose who you spend your time with.

Whether that's mentors, friends or good listeners who'll seek to understand without judging you or trying to fix you. And don't spend time with people who drain your energy. *You* need your energy!

6. Be assertive.

This is a key skill. You need assertiveness skills for all interactions. It will help you understand behaviour and enable you to choose what to say and how to say it in order to get better results.

7. Don't poison your body.

Tune in to what your body needs – and doesn't need. Caffeine? Alcohol? Cigarettes? Dairy? Sugar? You know best what your body thrives on. Don't underestimate the value of a healthy body as a stress-buster.

8. Take responsibility.

Take control of your life and own your problems and your ability to solve them. And don't compare yourself with others. The grass is always greener on the other side? Maybe: maybe not. Make *your* grass greener on *this* side by making decisions and taking action.

9. Music and meditation.

Listening to music can change your mood very quickly. Learning to meditate can change your life! Check out Peter Russell and his online course. Only 20 minutes a day is necessary. I tried his 5-week programme (I've tried many!) and I think it's excellent.

10. Take five minutes a day just for you.

Remind yourself what you love about your life. Stop what you are doing. Take pleasure in *this* moment right now. Think of a loved one. Look at a blue sky. Take five deep breaths. Be grateful for something. Smile at the next five people you see. *This* is your life – right here and right now. Breathe it in!

Ways to deal with potential stressors

To finish this chapter I've put together some ways you could deal with those stressors that we identified at the beginning. Take a look back at the items you ticked and check if there's something here that can help you right now.

I meet few women in positions similar to mine.

You have to find them! If not in your workplace, join a local women's network. You are not alone. Professional women are often starved of the company of other professional women. And it's not about finding someone to moan with (that's what friends are for), it's about talking about issues to do with work as well as life and knowing that you're talking the same language. I'm a great believer in women's networks. Try a few out if you haven't done so already.

I am too tired to cope with my family's needs.

If your family are little ones this is hard – their demands know no bounds. And there will be times like babies teething or children being sick when we just have to bite the bullet and get through it. So what I would ask is: are you the only one who *can* meet the needs? What about your partner? And as your children get older are you teaching them to take some responsibility for their own lives or are you still doing things for them that they are perfectly capable of doing for themselves?

I can't relax at home because there is too much to do.

Well, there *will* be too much to do if you are the only one doing it. Delegate to your children; yes you *can* do this. Tell them it's all about family contribution: you are providing the finances so they also have to make a contribution to make sure that your little community runs smoothly too. And put yourself on the job list. If **you** fold up the whole thing will probably come to a shuddering stop so it's in *everyone's* interest to make sure you keep healthy and sane. Schedule some time that is for *you* – whether it's every day or every week – make sure it's scheduled and that everybody knows it's scheduled. They won't take your needs seriously if you don't.

I am expected to take work home.

Whose expectations are these? Your manager's? Your own? Is this just what everyone does? You *are* entitled to a life outside of work. Maybe you could discuss with your manager what the expectations are around this. The problem with taking work home regularly is that people will get used to your output rate then it's really difficult to cut back. Maybe you need to renegotiate your workload. Is this possible?

I have most of the responsibility for running the home.

Unfortunately, this is the lot of most working women. People might help but we are the ones who know what needs to be done and organise it. This might suit you (at least you'll know it is all organised properly) but at least delegate whatever you can – to partners, children, delivery services, machines. Just get rid of the tasks!

I feel guilty if I am late home.

It's inevitable that you'll be home late sometimes. Explain this to your children. As long as there is some provision for them there is nothing to feel guilty about. You are a career woman *as well as* a mother. Your children need to understand this.

I have to prove to myself that I am a super partner/mother/manager.

First of all: you have *nothing* to prove. Wanting to prove something means you are needing to convince yourself of your worth. Raise your self-esteem and *know* that you are fine. Secondly, there is no such thing as a "super" anything and if you try to be any of these things you are setting yourself up for disappointment or even failure. And thirdly, you don't *need* to be a "super" anything. Sometimes a "good enough" something is just fine.

I have to prove to others that I am a super mother/partner/manager.

No you don't! And, even if you try, you have *no* control over what others think of you. What people think of you is their business. It's what you think of yourself that matters.

I work extra hard at being a good mother/partner to make up for the time I'm at work.

You already work really hard, right? You are a career woman *and* a wife/partner/ mother and you work hard at all your roles. And *all* your roles are important. There is absolutely no need to work extra hard or to make up for anything.

I have no/hardly any time to myself.

You are the only one who can change this. It is imperative that you make yourself a priority. If you don't you can be sure no one else will. And if you fall apart everything else will too.

I feel people are waiting for me to say that I can't cope.

Maybe this is true; maybe this is in your mind. If you feel this it may well be that you have set yourself impossibly high standards. If you are feeling particularly stressed then ask for help. You don't have to struggle on your own.

If the house doesn't run perfectly I get the blame.

Who blames you? The rest of the household? I think it's the responsibility of everyone who lives there to contribute to the smooth running of the household. Your children can't make a financial contribution to the household but they can contribute in other ways: tidying up, cooking, clearing up, ironing. It's not your job to make sure everything is running smoothly – it's *everyone's* job!

If the house doesn't run perfectly I accept the blame.

See last answer. Make some changes!

My family don't take my work seriously.

Everyone in the family has their own life, their own problems, their own priorities. The issue for women is that we put everyone's else's priorities before our own. Let the others know (and that includes extended family members) that your work is very important to you and that they are very important to you and that somehow you all have to fit everything in – it's not just up to you.

My friends don't want to talk about my work.

If your friends don't understand a lot about your job then they won't really want to talk about it – or be able to help you much anyway. See your friends as an important distraction to work and welcome it. I have a good friend who talks about her work a lot and while I have some understanding of what she does I don't always want to be talking to her about it. Your friends are great for laughing with, crying with, eating out with, going to the cinema with, shopping with… Who wants to talk with friends about work anyway. That's what your women's networks are for.

My family would prefer me not to work.

Maybe *you* would prefer you not to work. But with bills and mortgages to pay, **not** working may well be becoming a luxury. Of course children need to understand the financial advantages of your working. But it isn't always about money. I also think that it's important that children realise that it's important for *you* that you work because it gives you immense satisfaction, fulfils you and makes you happy. And if you're happy then there's a much better chance that everyone in the family will be too.

I'm always justifying that the family isn't suffering because I work.

Who to I wonder? Yourself? Other family members? Other women? It's a sad state that the tensions between women who work and those who stay home to care for children are often greater than tensions between women and men. Each group of women feels judged by the other. Women at home feel they have to justify why they have chosen to do so (which sounds like criticism of those women who work). Women who work feel they have to justify how their children don't suffer (which can sound like criticism of women who stay home). Women should be supporting each other whatever they choose. And none of us needs to justify ourselves – to anyone!

Hardy, Healthy, Happy action plan

Look back at the vulnerability to stress exercise, the reactions to stress exercise, the short-term strategies to cope with stress, the 10 quick tips for thriving not surviving and write here **specific** actions you are going to do. You can work on a one week, one month or 3-month plan – whatever works for you. Use your notebook to do your plan then monitor your actions. You can update the plan every week or month.

Part 3
Taking Action

Chapter 7

Stand Up and Speak Out

This area is perhaps what gives us most stress! Will I make a fool of myself in meetings? How can I stop being so nervous before a presentation? Sometimes, our heart races and our palms begin to sweat just thinking about that talk we have to do. Don't worry! This chapter is going to ease your nerves and give you confidence.

In this chapter:

- ▸ How to give great talks and presentations
- ▸ Improving presentation weaknesses
- ▸ 10 ways to be effective in meetings

How to give great talks and presentations

For every talk or presentation you have sat through and enjoyed, there are probably 10 others you can't even remember. Perhaps you were bored or distracted, or even lost your way in a maze of jargon and technicalities. The ability to present information to an audience in a clear, confident and coherent way is one of the fundamental skills required in organisations today.

Self-Reflection 1

What's your worst fear(s) about giving talks and presentations?

Here are the key characteristics of a good speaker.
Great speakers:

- Look confident
- Keep to the point
- Have interesting content presented in a logical order
- Are entertaining
- Don't speak in a monotone
- Make good use of visual aids
- Speak clearly and simply
- Smile and make eye contact with different people in the audience
- Answer questions
- Don't overrun

Some of these characteristics relate to how you look, some to how you speak, and some to what you say. So let's break this down some more and start first with the non-verbal communication. We're starting here because it actually carries the most impact.

When we meet someone new we quickly gain an impression of what the other person is like. We start to make up a story about them almost immediately. Whether or not we want to, we communicate and read information about important issues such as confidence, competence, status and compatibility. We do this partly through what is said, but mostly through our non-verbal communication.

Research studies show that we make up our minds about each other in the first few minutes of meeting and find it very difficult to change our minds. Indeed, one of the latest studies shows that the first 3-4 seconds are the most crucial. Gender, colour, height and also our choices on signals such as dress, posture, gestures, and eye contact will almost at once be woven into perceptions of who they think we are.

We may intend to be very professional, but how is our image being interpreted? What is it like to be on the receiving end of us?

Most communication is inaccurate in that it's unlikely to be received in precisely the way it was intended by the sender. We need to give others as much help as possible to "read" us in the way we want to be seen. They will still be making assumptions, but they could be closer to what we want to say and who we feel we really are.

So we have some choices to make about how we want to come across.

We first collect information from:

- **Physical characteristics**

  Then we gain more insight by analysing …

- **Vocal qualities**

  And only after that do we pay attention to the…

- **Words**

  Many research studies on both sides of the Atlantic confirm what the rational brain at first resists: that non-verbal signals are at least four times as important as the words we use.

Michael Argyle (who was a pioneer of social psychology in Britain and broke new ground with his studies of non-verbal communication and social skills) says: *'People give four times as much weight to non-verbal than to verbal signals.'*

Argyle is not saying that our words are not important. The verbal content may well be crucial, but the intended meaning can be overturned by the non-verbal element of the communication.

In summary, our communication, words, body language and voice must all carry the same message for us to have any hope of being understood.

The best way to improve non-verbal communication is to raise our awareness and simultaneously release any tension. We must be honest, natural and authentic to avoid the sort of miscommunication that could cause us to be perceived as incongruent or negative in the first place.

So let's look at 10 non-verbal factors that give high credibility.

Good volume and resonant tone

People using good volume and tone are considered to be enthusiastic, sincere, proud, interesting, dependable and energetic.

Conversational style

This is perceived as intelligent, sophisticated, calm, friendly, sincere, reasonable, confident and generally more people orientated.

Visual images and vivid language

These are used to evoke response. For most people visual images are the most memorable.

Pace

The rate of speech can vary from 120 to 195 words per minute. Credibility is diminished below 110 and sense disappears over 210. Research shows a preference for moderate to fast speakers.

Clarity

Good articulation is perceived to be trustworthy, sincere, considerate, energised and intelligent.

Variety

Building in vocal variety is essential. Attention is controlled by a deep part of the brain and is switched off by repetitive stimuli. Consider also that we can think at four times the rate at which we speak, so it is necessary to continually keep the audience attentive.

Eye contact

This can vary. In a Western culture high levels of eye contact are linked to sincerity, trustworthiness and friendliness. Generally 60-95% is perceived as positive.

Facial expression

For reflecting the verbal content, illustrating commitment, interest, emphasis appropriately. Smiling and nodding are among the most persuasive and compelling.

Gestures

Should be open and energised but without being repetitive, jerky or hesitant. Relaxed movements showing palms can be persuasive and will help keep attention.

Movement

Must reflect relaxation, energy and commitment to the focus of the communication.

Self-Reflection 2

Think about great speakers you have seen. What do they do really well that you wish you could do?

Now what about low credibility factors? There are more of these!

Formality

Perceived as a barrier to persuasive communication unless absolutely essential.

Speech disturbances

Including repetitions, omissions, slips of the tongue, grammatical errors. Words like "kind of" and "sort of" are perceived to relate to lack of competence and intelligence.

High pitch

Perceived as nervous, less truthful/reliable, less potent.

Breathiness

Perceived as insincere and boring.

Lack of vocal variety

Perceived as dull, boring, cold and withdrawn.

Harsh tone

Perceived as anxious, unattractive and inflexible.

Over articulation

Perceived as fussy and uncompromising.

Lazy articulation

Perceived as careless, bored or insincere.

Tension in body posture

Such as raised or hunched shoulders, is perceived as nervousness and makes the listeners nervous too

Jerky and/or hesitant movements

Show nervousness and a lack of confidence.

Relaxation without energy

Perceived as lack of interest and carelessness as in a slumped posture.

Mannerisms

Such as neck scratching, nose or ear rubbing, fiddling or biting will diminish credibility as they interrupt the impression of clear, direct and confident communication.

Face touching and head down

Covering the mouth or touching the nose with a hand can be perceived as anxiety or even a lie.

Stress signals

These can include upper chest breathing, blushing, shaking, sweating, rubbing palms together etc. They encourage the listener to doubt the speaker.

Facial expressions

Including looking over-serious, frowning, or facial expressions that are incongruent or immovable are likely to bore the listener or make them feel uncomfortable.

Eye contact

20- 40% eye contact is perceived as low credibility.

Self-Reflection 3

Think about a talk you gave that went really well. Why do you think this was? And what about a talk that went really badly?

As with everything – the more you practise, the better you will get. And the very best way to increase your confidence is to be well prepared. So let's look at that next.

Most experienced speakers freely admit that careful preparation is their secret. The more time you spend preparing, the more likely it is to go well. So let's look at some questions to help you. If you have a talk coming up soon you can use the Talk Preparation Sheet at the end of this section to help you.

What is your title?

The first thing to think about is the title. Think of something catchy, something that will grab people's attention even before you have started.

When you are going to give it?

The next thing is to consider when you are going to give it. Not only will the amount of preparation time affect any research you might want to carry out, but it will also affect the preparation of any visual aids and the amount of practice time you can allow.

Why you are giving it?

This is really important and is often overlooked. Are you being asked to speak because you are an expert on the subject? Are you speaking to a report you have completed? Are you trying to influence a decision to be made about something? Are you just filling a spot on someone else's agenda? Being very clear about your objective will mean you can frame your talk accordingly.

I once gave a presentation to small business owners and prepared my talk with a clear objective of positioning myself as an experienced business owner and offering a programme right at the end to help business owners develop their business. Unfortunately, I didn't realise until I arrived that in fact this Small Business Association were having their AGM and I was just put in as a guest speaker on the night. People had gone for the meeting, not because they were interested in me or my topic. Had I realised that I would have slanted the talk very differently. So as well as defining your objective you need to be clear about the objective of the person who asked you.

Who will your audience be?

Again, this is really important. Are they your peers? Your superiors? How much do they already know about the subject? How deep can you go? If you are one speaker in a series, what kind of talks are they used to? How personal can you be? Did they choose to come to your talk or were they required to attend? You need to find out something about your audience so you can make sure you pitch your talk at the right level.

What final impression do you want to leave them with?

What do you want them to do or think about as a result of hearing your talk? Are you trying to influence them or just inform them? What thought do you want to leave them with? It could be:

- *I'll buy one tomorrow.*
- *We're right on plan to meet our targets.*
- *This sounds interesting; I think I'll go on that trip they are planning in two weeks.*
- *We need to rethink this before making a decision.*
- *We need to introduce this scheme in this company.*

Some time spent thinking about the audience and the impression you want to leave them with can make all the difference between your talk being memorable or forgettable.

How long will it last?

Find out the length of your slot and don't overrun, especially if there are speakers following you. And find this out before you prepare. There is nothing worse than preparing an hour's talk and then finding out at the event that you only have 20 minutes. Also find out if the organiser expects you to answer questions at the end. If so, leave time for this. I would always recommend that you let the audience know if you are going to allow questions at the end but not during your presentation. Otherwise you can be sidetracked, thrown off balance and lose a lot of time. And speaking of time, remember, if you are using visual aids, the talk will take longer than you think it will.

Where will you be giving the talk?

If it is an internal presentation then you might already be familiar with the room. If not then you want to be sure about the size, seating, lighting, heating, ventilation and access to electricity points. If it is an external talk and you can't visit the venue beforehand then make sure you are clear about the address and route and arrive in plenty of time to see the room and test the equipment. It's always a good idea to give the organiser a sheet with your requirements on e.g. if you have a choice do you prefer people sitting in rows or at round tables; if the room requires you to have a microphone ask for a lapel one if you don't want to be holding one; decide if you need roving microphones for audience contributions; can your slides be seen even in a lit room. Personally I don't like it when I am speaking and the lights in the room are dimmed. I need to see the faces and eyes of the audience or I can't interact with them.

What do you want to say?

This is the most important part. Aim to break your content down into six or seven key ideas, which will form the framework for your presentation. Don't forget the well-known sales adage: 'Tell them what you're going to tell them; tell them; then tell them what you've told them.' It's sound advice. Before you fill in the detail it might be a good idea to show the key ideas to the person who asked you to give the talk. Better to find out now that they wanted a different thread.

After you have your key ideas sorted out, you need to identify some key words for each idea. This will ensure that you keep your focus on the central issues and it will be these key words that you have on your prompt cards to glance at during your talk.

How will you say it?

There are two things to consider. Firstly, are you going to read it, learn it, or speak freely using prompt cards or slides?

Some people feel more confident writing out their speech in full and reading it. However, the major problem with this is that there is a big difference between the written and the spoken word. If you read from a written document it can sound false and wooden. And if you're looking at the document you are reading then you're not looking at your audience. They might start to wonder why they bothered to come. And your voice might not carry so well because your head is down.

I always feel cheated if I turn up for a presentation and someone reads it out. Why didn't they just email it out? I want to see something of the person and the personality. I want to feel their energy and their passion. It's very hard to convey this if you are reading from a written script.

Try to get into the habit of talking rather than reading a speech. Use small cue cards that you can hold and that have your key ideas and key words on. Number the points you want to make and put your key words in large letters or another colour. You can number your cue cards or attach them together at one corner and just peel off each one as you finish your points.

The second point to consider is how you make the best use of visual aids. In some organisations everyone who gives a talk or presentation is expected to use a slide presentation and people are used to sitting through tens of slides for each talk. If you have a lot of figures to present in graphs and charts then clearly this is the best way. Slides can also show your key points so they act as cue cards that you can speak to. It's also useful to include visual aids if you are nervous about the attention being on you the whole time. It's all about preparing your data in an interesting and varied way to avoid the risk of your audience getting bored or losing concentration. For large audiences, slides and video shorts are probably the best way unless you are speaking personally; then all you need is your impactful self. But don't use too many slides. I have seen talks where there would be 20-40 slides for a 40-minute talk so the presenter is whizzing through the last few and I am left wondering what I might have missed.

Six things to remember when using visual aids:

1. Use them to summarise, support or emphasise. Remember you are going to talk to the points on the slides, not just read them out.

2. Use colour and pictures to make things clearer and more interesting. Your slides have to keep people entertained as well as informing them.

3. Keep them simple. Many times I have seen that people put way too much information on their slides. The slides are for the key points, not all the text.

4. Make sure to be clear about which slides are linked to the aspects of your talk and put the slide number on the cue card so you know when to move on to the next one.

5. If you are not going to send the organiser your presentation on a USB stick, don't forget to find out how your laptop will link with the projector. Try and have a run through before your talk. This is especially important if you are using music or a video as part of your presentation. There is nothing worse than reaching a critical point where you want to play a high impact video clip and there is a deafening silence.

6. Provide copies of your key points for members of the audience if the numbers are not too large but if possible keep them to the end or people will be reading through them instead of listening to you.

Use the form on the next page to plan the next talk you are going to give.

Talk Preparation Sheet

Title of talk
When is the talk?
Why am I giving the talk?
Who will my audience be?
What final impression do I want them to have?
How long will the talk last?

Where am I giving the talk?

What do I want to say?

Key Ideas	*Key Words*	*Visual Aids*

Self-Reflection 4

What aspect of preparing a talk do you think you could improve?

So now you have prepared your talk but you need to practise. The importance of practising can't be over emphasised. However good your preparation is you will be judged on your actual performance. Practice can help you to control your nerves, and thus control your voice.

Nerves affect different people in different ways. You may appear aggressive and speak too loudly; your mouth may dry up making it difficult to swallow and breathe; your mind might go completely blank; you may feel unable to speak louder than normal for sustained periods or you may speak far too quickly. One sure way your nerves will show is through your voice. If you can control your voice you can control your nerves – or at least give that impression.

So let's look at voice control.

There are three main ways to practise voice control all of which will help you to become familiar with the content of your presentation and get your timing right.

1. Practise on your own.
See and use the key words on your cue cards; firstly to find phrases and expressions which sound right for you and secondly to make sure you use your visual aids at the right points.

2. Tape yourself.
Listen to your voice speed, make sure the pitch is right and that your voice is not strained when you speak louder than usual. Someone I know practised this way and realised that she took little in-breaths every now and again which were very irritating to the listener. She didn't realise she was doing this until she heard herself back on tape.

3. Deliver the talk to a friend.
Get feedback on content, visual aids, voice control and body language.

Once you have a lot of talks under your belt and get more comfortable doing them you will find you don't need to practise first.

Self-Reflection 5

What kind of feedback have you received when you've given presentations?

There is one more point that is really important to mention if your talk is intended to influence people, and that is the research around what motivates people who you are trying to influence.

It shows that people are motivated by habit, emotion and reason – in that order.

Habit

The most powerful. As a persuasive lever you could suggest:

- Others are already changing; we may be left out. Or...
- That any change will be a small extension of what happens now.

Emotion

Noticeably stronger in groups. You can use it in a variety of ways:

- To appeal to instincts for self-preservation: protect the family, one's job, the group, organisation or company. To promote future stability.
- To appeal by offering material benefits and pride of acquisition and ownership. Or...
- By illustrating the contrary suggestion: creating doubts, showing alternatives to be poor, making the future look bleak, playing on fears and dangers. This is powerful, but actually could be a potentially self-defeating strategy in disempowering people in the long run.

Reason

People like to think they are guided by intellect and logic, but research shows reason to be least powerful of the motivating forces. Apparently many people cannot distinguish between a factual statement and an inferred statement, which is based on perceptions not facts.

One of our most powerfully developed faculties is what psychologists call **rationalisation**: we can always find a reason for what the emotions dictate. To harness this in persuasive speech we must combine reasonable and emotional arguments, e.g. use reason to appeal to the emotions.

I coached someone once who was quite brilliant at talking about facts and figures and always presented a reasoned, well thought out argument but he wasn't passionate about his subject. He wasn't inspiring his people. People aren't inspired by facts and figures they are inspired by people. He had to start speaking from his heart; showing his people his heart and his passion. Once he engaged them emotionally his reason could come to the fore. The more up the leadership ladder you go, the more you will be called on to inspire with your presentations so never be afraid to speak from your heart.

Improving presentation weaknesses

Now with the best will in the world, however well prepared you are, things can still go wrong. Here are some tips.

I never know what to do with my hands. It must be very irritating for people I'm talking to.

Action points:

- Make sure that you hold something in your hands – cue cards or a pen.
- If you sit, keep your hands loosely together on your knee.
- If nervousness is causing you to wave your hands about, take some slow deep breaths to calm yourself down before you start.

When I'm talking, I suddenly become aware that everyone's listening to me – then my mind goes completely blank.

Action points:

- If you have prepared well, you will have all your main points written on cue cards. A glance at the next one should bring you on to your next point immediately.
- Take a sip of water to buy yourself some time.
- Tell the audience that your mind has gone blank and ask someone to remind you of the last thing you said. It can happen to anyone. People like honesty and the audience will be more comfortable with this approach and empathise with you. I have done this myself!

I haven't got a naturally loud voice and find it difficult to speak louder when I'm giving a talk.

Action points:

- Practise five minutes of your talk at a time in a louder voice than usual and gradually increase the time until you can talk for half an hour without feeling strained.
- If possible, use a microphone.

When I'm nervous I tend to speak too quickly, which can make it difficult for people to follow what I say and I know I can appear aggressive when I'm talking about something I feel strongly about, and this alienates my listeners.

Action points:

- Deliberately pause between each point you want to make.
- Speak in a deeper voice than usual and more slowly.
- A sign of aggression is using the hands forcefully, pointing for instance. Hold your hands loosely or hold something.

I prefer to avoid eye contact with my listeners, so it's difficult to establish a rapport with them. I like to read out my prepared speech word for word.

Action points:

- Ask someone to observe where you are looking. Is it above the audience, or to one particular side, or at the person who nods at what you say?
- Practise looking at someone different every time you look up, even if it's only for a second.
- Practise eye contact in everything you do – when ordering a coffee or speaking to a sales assistant. Get used to looking into people's eyes.

I find it difficult to relax in a formal setting and I make others nervous too.

Action points:

- Use an open body posture.
- Smile and speak in a steady manner.
- Take some slow deep breaths before you start.

I'm apprehensive about the questions at the end of a talk. I'm always afraid I'll be asked something I can't answer.

Action points:

- Remember that you will probably anticipate the questions if you prepare your talk well.
- Prepare additional material if you think you might need it.
- Throw the question open and ask the audience for their comments.
- Run through your talk with a typical audience member to check if there are likely to be questions you hadn't thought of.

- If you don't know the answer, say so, but also say you will find out and get back to them (then make sure you do). Or tell them where they could find the information.
- If you really don't want to take questions in the public forum, offer to discuss questions individually and informally after the session.

I'm bound to make a fool of myself. Anyway, I haven't got anything interesting to say.

Action points:

- Lots of people hate giving presentations; don't set yourself up to be perfect.
- Recognise that it is normal to feel anxious and tell yourself that you can control your nerves by breathing correctly and taking sips of water.
- Remember that it does get easier with practice.
- Remember that you have been invited to speak because someone thinks you have important things to say so believe them!
- People who are sitting in your audience are wanting you to do well; they are on your side. And they are interested in what you are there to talk about.
- Instead of telling yourself negative statements, try positive ones instead. You can! You will! And do not apologise for anything.

Self-Reflection 6

How do you think you can improve your talks and presentations?

10 ways to be effective in meetings

Finally we are going to look at meetings. As a manager and as a leader, much of your time will be spent in meetings of one kind or another and it is in your interests to play your part in improving their effectiveness.

Self-Reflection 7

What percentage of your time is spent in meetings? Are you happy with that?
What kinds of meetings are they?

Good meetings do not just happen; they are made. The most ineffectual meetings are those which have no apparent purpose, those where no one speaks, and those which are badly chaired. In other words: meetings for meetings' sake. A meeting must have a clearly defined purpose; if it does not, it should never take place at all. The three main purposes of meetings are:

1. To communicate information e.g. team meetings
2. To solve problems e.g. management meetings
3. To make decisions e.g. strategy meetings

Of course, meetings might combine two or all three of these purposes. They are a useful means of creating a sense of identity and cementing relationships in a team that may not meet on a day-to-day basis. They provide a structured forum for dissent and enable problems to be nipped in the bud.

Attendees who contribute positively place more value on the decisions that are made and have more commitment to their successful implementation. Meetings are a good way to brainstorm, as people share experiences and expertise. If handled properly, they can be motivating for teams and rewarding for managers.

As a woman you may well be in the minority in some meetings especially as you go higher and higher in leadership, and anything that you do or say will be scrutinised by the other participants. Your confidence and competence will be assessed on your behaviour during the meeting.

Listen to what these women have said about being in the minority at a meeting. Do any of these comments strike a chord with you?

I was at a meeting to discuss the new building programme and I happened to be the only woman there. At one point I expressed concern at the projected staffing levels and my comment was ignored. I knew it was a valid point because I'd discussed it with the planners.

I attended a meeting with senior management where the main item on the agenda was a policy change that would affect working practices in my department. I opposed the change, and, although I knew that others felt the same as I did, I was the only one who voted in this way.

I had to chair the meeting as my boss was on leave. One of the men didn't like this at all. He couldn't resist the temptation to be sarcastic and make me look foolish.

One of the problems of being a woman in management and leadership positions is that you may find yourself in the minority. This may put you at a disadvantage in a number of situations. Meetings are a good example of this when women often find they are not taken seriously. It is often the case that he who shouts loudest and longest wins in the end, and some women find it a struggle to make their voice heard in the same way.

You may find that the type of supportive behaviour you would receive from other women allowing you to express your views is lacking in a predominantly male atmosphere. This can be intimidating for many women, who may respond in one of two ways. Either they may remain silent, confirming their lack of worth (or interest) in the eyes of the male majority, or they may compensate for an apparent lack of power by behaving aggressively. Neither of these responses works. The woman concerned will be ineffectual at the meeting. Moreover, she will be **seen** to be ineffectual.

What often happens is that men dominate the proceedings and have more success in making their opinions known and considered.

Self-Reflection 8

Think back to the last few meetings you attended. Describe any problems you had in speaking up; putting forward your ideas; influencing others' opinions or influencing the way the meeting progressed.

So how can you be effective in meetings?

Firstly, you have a 3-fold responsibility to be effective in meetings.

1. To your team to represent their interests and views.
2. To the other members of the meeting to ensure its effectiveness – everyone has a duty to participate.
3. To yourself to promote opinions, ideas and needs, which you believe to be important and worthy of consideration.

Here are the 10 ways to be most effective in meetings.

1. Listen actively.

Concentrate on what is being said, rather than on your response. Good listening leads to good questioning, improves group understanding, and keeps the meeting good humoured.

Sometimes people prepare what they are going to say and then wait for an appropriate moment to intervene. Consequently, they do not listen to other speakers. Participate fully in the discussion by listening actively. This is something that many people fail to do, and it leads to many misunderstandings and much time-wasting.

If you feel that you need to prepare what you are going to say, jot down a few words on paper — and then tune in fully to what is being said.

2. Ask questions if you don't understand.

Women, in particular, are often misled into believing that everyone else (except them) understands what is going on. They may feel that by asking questions they are exposing ignorance, and that this displays vulnerability. There is no disgrace in asking for clarification of points that may be ambiguous or unclear. You will probably find that other people have been as unsure as you if you ask 'Are you saying that...?' or 'What exactly do you mean by...?' Asking a question is also a useful way of gaining confidence before coming in at a later stage to state your point of view.

3. Be confronting *and* supportive.

Many women dislike debate and argument because they feel that by opposing another person's point of view they are rejecting that person. Remember that you have the right to state your viewpoint, even if it goes against those of other people at the meeting. Indeed, as a manager or leader, you have a responsibility to participate on your own behalf, and on behalf of your team.

Even if you disagree with what is being said, recognise and respect the right of other speakers to voice their point of view. Support does not have to be verbal: nods, smiles and other examples of non-verbal behaviour indicate agreement. But remember, if you always show what you are thinking non-verbally, people will be less inclined to ask your opinion. So voice your support of others by saying things like:

- *That's a good idea.*
- *I agree with John when he said...*
- *Although I can understand why you feel that way, I support Mary when she says that...*

Your support is thus likely to be appreciated, remembered, and reciprocated.

4. Speak clearly, honestly and directly.

When putting forward your point of view do not be afraid of saying 'I'. Be more concerned with what you are saying than how other people are reacting to you. Try not to let anxieties about your behaviour affect the way in which you present your point of view. On the whole, people are less likely to be aware of your nerves than you think they are.

5. Do not let others interrupt you.

It is easy to back down and stop speaking when you are interrupted, particularly if the other person is louder, aggressive or more senior. What makes it perhaps more difficult is the fact that such intervention disrupts your mental flow, and you may lose your train of thought. Some people react to interruptions by continuing to speak, but louder. Others find it easier to draw attention to the interruption by asking to be allowed to continue.

And if you find it difficult to find a gap in the debate to put forward your point of view, try not to intervene by interrupting another speaker. Attract the attention of the Chairperson to the fact that you wish to speak.

6. Keep your contributions positive, short and to the point.

The people who achieve most at meetings are often those who say little but listen carefully, and who have planned their contribution. Much time is wasted in discussions by people who speak at length as a power ploy or in order to score points over another participant. You will appreciate the attempts made by other people to be brief and concise; therefore try to do so yourself.

7. Use non-verbal communication to reinforce what you say.

When you speak in a meeting, pay attention to the manner in which you speak and how you appear. A confident voice and demeanour will reinforce the impact of what you are saying. Note also the following points:

- Speak audibly
- Vary the tone of your voice. You are more likely to hold people's attention this way
- Don't smile when making a serious point, or laugh after you have made it
- Make sure that everyone can see and hear you. Move to another place if they can't, e.g. stand up or move to the end of the table
- Don't fidget; it distracts others from what you are saying

8. Ask for a response to your contribution, if you don't get one.

If you feel your point has been glossed over, request a response:

- *I feel that this is the case. Does this point of view have any support?*
- *How do other people feel about this suggestion?*
- *I feel that the points I made are worthy of consideration. Do I need to expand on them?*

9. Don't back down just because people don't accept what you say.

If you don't have confidence in yourself, it is easy to be swayed by someone else's point of view. Allow yourself some time to consider the merits of other people's arguments before rejecting your own.

10. Always make a contribution.

Make sure you contribute something to every meeting you attend even if it's only to ask a question or support another speaker. You are at that meeting because it is connected with your role. If you aren't going to contribute, what are you doing there? Although this is number 10 on this list it's the one I really want you to remember.

If you managed to identify some things that you can do, make sure that you put them into practice at the next meeting you attend.

If you have never contributed very much in the past, take things slowly and remember that you are not suddenly going to change the habits of a lifetime overnight. When you have carried out one of your intentions, evaluate it afterwards. Ask yourself, 'How was I? How could I improve next time?' If you have a friend or colleague whom you can trust and rely upon for a fair opinion, ask this person to help you to assess your performance.

If you feel that your contribution to meetings is good, positive and difficult to improve on, ask yourself how you could help the meetings you attend to run more smoothly for everyone present. Bear in mind that, as with most things in life, what you get out of a meeting will usually be in direct proportion to what you put in. Like most skills, being effective in meetings does come easier with practice.

Meetings are an important forum for women to exercise influence, and to get themselves noticed. As a woman with her sights set on the next step of the promotional ladder, you should realise that meetings can play a key role in gaining you visibility, credibility and respect for your competence and confident behaviour.

Self-Reflection 9

How do you think you can improve your effectiveness in meetings?

Chapter 8

The Positive Path to Promotion

Getting a promotion is a tricky thing. Of course you wanted the job but now
maybe there are hardly any women at your level and you feel isolated. And
everyone seems to have different expectations about how you should be.
How do you establish yourself in your new role?
And how do you plan for the next one?

In this chapter:

- ▸ Coping with mixed messages
- ▸ Dealing with role pressures
- ▸ A 9-point action plan for the successful professional woman
- ▸ Five key actions to remember about yourself

Coping with mixed messages

L et's start by looking at some mixed messages that you might get from people, in particular your managers, as you move into a leadership position. These are messages that your male peers might not get.

Take risks but be consistently outstanding

Part of leadership is about taking risks. Being creative and innovative must involve taking risks and some research has actually shown that executive women are more likely than executive men to move in new and original directions so that's the good news.

Taking risks means that you will undoubtedly make some mistakes along the way. But if you're expected to be consistently outstanding then that doesn't leave much room for making mistakes. So get used to wins and losses. Make sure people know that you're being creative and taking risks, and certainly let them know about your successes. And if you do make a mistake then deal with it quickly and let people know what you are going to do to correct it.

Be tough but don't be macho

We looked a lot at masculine and feminine styles in Chapter 2 so this is just a reminder that being tough and decisive isn't the same as being aggressive and unfeeling. As always, keep a balance between both ends of the spectrum. We're going to look at this issue of becoming like a man (or not!) in a moment.

Take responsibility but follow my advice

This is a tough one. Of course you have not only to make decisions but also take responsibility for them. And it's always good to get advice. Women generally are good at gathering feedback and advice. This is fine, but recognise that some people won't understand what you are up to (often because you are saying something new and ahead of your time). Also it seems that executive women are more likely than executive men to be given advice from senior men and expected to take it. If you are following others' advice all the time then you aren't making decisions on your own that you can take responsibility for.

Watch out to see if you are being given these mixed messages and think about how you are going to weave your diplomatic way through the maze.

Self-Reflection 1

Have you had any of these mixed messages? What about other messages that you think your male counterparts don't get?

Dealing with role pressures

Now let's suppose you get a promotion and you're delighted. You're putting in long hours to establish yourself quickly. You're getting to know your team and your first quarterly results are due; you're excited. And yet, you are aware of some things going on that you hadn't bargained for and you're starting to feel the pressure...

Here are five role pressures you might be facing and what you can do.

1. Being the token woman.

You realised that the higher up the scale you went the fewer women you would have around you and you knew that you were moving to a traditionally male environment. But you didn't really expect to be hearing the whispers and insinuations that you only got the job because you are a woman and you don't know how to counter them.

There will always be people who will say that and the tiny minority at the end of the scale who are prepared to be antagonistic to you are unlikely to change no matter what you do. So don't waste your time trying to change them but don't tolerate rude or uncooperative behavior. Establish guidelines quickly for appropriate and inappropriate behaviour and make sure everyone knows them. As for the others you have two options: address the comments openly at a team meeting, say you don't appreciate them and you expect the highest performance from your team and they can expect the same from you. Or ignore the comments and know you will win people round with your commitment, your leadership style and your results.

And never doubt your own competence and ability to do the job. You've worked hard for your promotion and you know you deserve it. Do not allow anyone to affect your self-esteem. They need your permission for this. Don't give it.

2. Being isolated.

You look around you and there are no other women at your level. There's nothing wrong with the guys; you like working with men. But you are starting to feel a bit like an alien. They talk about different things; they rarely mention their families; and you seem to see things very differently to them. There are more and more discussions where you seem to be the odd one out. It's like there are some rules that you didn't know...

This is where women's networking really comes into its own. There are many women at your level of seniority, with your skills and talents, who see the world through similar lenses, whose brains work in similar ways, who may be in the same industry, they just don't necessarily work in your organisation. So you have to find out where they are. Check out both online and offline networks. Talk to women like yourself who have similar concerns and approaches. It's not that you're looking for agreement on everything. It's just that you want to feel you are in a territory where you can speak and understand the language. Of course we need to be careful about polarisation between the genders. But, as we have seen, there are male/female differences that we would be foolish to ignore and you need support now so you need to find women who can support you. Once there are equal numbers of men and women at senior levels you will have lots of choice about finding kindred spirits. Until then, you might need to go further afield to find them.

3. Being excluded.

You know the joke about decisions being made in the men's room and on the golf course... well it's not always a joke. Don't want to play squash at lunch or go to the bar on a Friday after work? Then unfortunately that means you might be excluded.

Men won't be doing these things intentionally in order to deliberately exclude you. They'll be doing them because that's what they do. And if you choose not to go then there's a good change that you won't be involved in important discussions.

Don't allow yourself to be excluded. Set up some social occasions that everyone can enjoy. Not all men like lunchtime exercise and some people in certain religions are unlikely to go to bars. You won't be the only one being excluded. Bring it up as a topic at a team meeting. Every organisation is committed to Inclusion as a policy so bring up the topic of inclusion and exclusion and look at how it is being implemented in your team. It is important to bring some of these issues to the surface and talk about them. Make the unconscious conscious then everyone can see the whole picture.

I'd like to think that the next one isn't an issue but unfortunately for some women it still is...

4. Resisting female gender roles.

Are you expected to be the one who pours the coffee? Takes the minutes? (Yes it does still happen.) And is it being petty and churlish to object?

No. And you must object, but in the right way. Because – whether you like it or not – you are a role model for women and I believe all women have a responsibility to the women coming up behind them to make things better. So if something needs to change then so much the better that it's you who helps to bring that change about. Changing people's stereotypical assumptions is a slow process of raising their awareness every time the stereotype shows itself. And there are effective but non-threatening ways to do it.

If you are expected to pour the coffee say, 'I'm happy to pour the coffee today because it will be a while then before it's my turn again.' And then make sure you don't pour again until others have taken a turn. Re the minutes you could say, 'Is there a volunteer to take the minutes or shall we take it in turns?'

You don't need to make a point about what you are not prepared to do and why – just suggest how you want it to work and then act accordingly.

Finally, there's one more thing to watch out for.

5. Becoming like a man.

Some women deliberately adopt the male characteristics they see being rewarded and resolve to change when they reach a position of real power. But it's difficult to swim with the sharks without becoming one. And it's hard to try and live like one if you're really a dolphin.

Every organisation says they want their people to bring their whole selves to work. Women have a great opportunity to bring forth their inner power and resources, their gifts and their perspectives and contribute to a new kind of leadership, which is sorely needed in our organisations. But to do this you need to be able to tap into your authentic self and have the courage not to compromise your personal values. There are women in very senior positions in organisations already doing this. Find out who they are and what they do. Use them as your role models. Ask one of them to mentor you. Your feminine power is so needed. Stay true to yourself and become more of who you are. That is how you will make your mark and help to create the organisations that every employee is dreaming of.

158

Self-Reflection 2

Have you faced any of these role pressures? Which ones?
How did you cope with them?

A 9-point action plan for the successful professional woman

For the final part of this chapter we're going to look at some specific actions you need to put in place to make sure your career develops the way you want it to.

1. Be the best.

Being good at your job isn't the only thing that matters, but your performance at your job is the first and most crucial requirement for achieving promotion. You won't be noticed or singled out if you are only average. Being the best involves commitment, energy and, above all, effort. Try to excel at what is important and leave the less important tasks to others. Being the best is vital for women because women often have to perform twice as well as men to be thought as good as men.

You don't just have to demonstrate your skills; you have to do so with enthusiasm. People who are keen and enthusiastic are the ones who get noticed. A lethargic or even grudging approach doesn't win approval or a promotion. So what can you do to demonstrate that you are the best at work?

Here are some questions for you to think about:

- **What is your particular area of expertise?** Identify it, make note of it, be clear about it.

- **Is there something in particular that only you can do?** This is very important because it helps you to position yourself as an expert in what you do.

- **What is the highest qualification in your field, and do you have it?** This will be important when you go for that next promotion.

- **Do your knowledge and expertise relate to a major aspect of the organisation's work?** The more closely your skills are linked to what is valued highly in the organisation, the better placed you are to be able to be seen to be doing a great job.

- **Do people frequently consult you and ask you for advice?** If not – who are they asking and why are they asking that person and not you? Your aim is for you to be the person who has the answers.

- **Are you the best person at your particular job and do people know this?** If you are the best at what you do and you are recognised as such, you are definitely in a position to move ahead. If you are not the best but want to be the best, then look at your requirements – whether they are training, development or additional opportunities.

If you are the best at what you do but not recognised as such, then you need to plan ways of demonstrating your skills. This could include taking on more high-profile tasks, writing more reports, highlighting your achievements or simply telling your manager what a great job you are doing.

2. Set goals for yourself.

If you don't know where you are going, then how are you going to know if you have arrived? Goals are like dreams with deadlines. Setting long-term goals for yourself will require some in-depth thinking about your work, your personal life, and your future. Ask yourself, 'What do I want to be doing in two years' time or five years' time or 12 months' time and what do I need to do now to achieve this?'

You should be doing something each day to achieve your goal, and attaining your goal must be on your list of priorities. If it isn't then, of course, you have little chance of achieving it. So once you have defined your goal, write it down, look at it regularly, modify it if necessary, and see if you can spend 5-10 minutes every day doing something directly linked to the goal you are reaching for.

3. Establish your priorities.

Negotiate home and work commitments with your partner and family. Your career is also a family affair. Involve them in some household responsibilities. We looked at this already in an earlier chapter.

4. Improve yourself.

You are going to need to take charge of your own self-development in order to succeed. Even when training schemes are available – especially management training schemes – the numbers of women who take advantage of them are still small, which is interesting. If you want to be considered for the next promotion, you need to make sure you are prepared. Look at yourself objectively in order to identify your skills and qualities. Make a list of your possible development areas and analyse them. See if any of them present potential handicaps at the next level on the ladder. After you have answered this question, you can decide whether you are prepared to change or whether you are happy to settle for less and settle for what you have got, which is fine too.

If you are looking at improving, once you have recognised the areas where you need to improve, look particularly at the skills needed at the next level and ask yourself what you are going to do to gain these skills. Look at people who have been promoted to similar jobs and look at what they can do that you can't. This should help you to start a self-development programme of your own – and you must start it on your own. Nobody is going to offer you training on a plate but if you need it, then do ask for it. Senior people need to see that you have all the necessary skills to operate at the next level before they can visualise you in the role. People often – and especially women – seem to not get that message that being good at what you do is very important, but in order for you to get that **next** job, someone who is hiring for that next job has to be able to visualise you in that role. So you need to do everything that you can to make it easy for them to see you in it.

Here are some questions you can ask yourself:

- *What are my areas for improvement?*
- *Where can I get the training or experience that I need?*
- *What am I going to do about it?*
- *When am I going to start?*

Talk to somebody already doing the job to find out what else you need to know and do.

5. Focus on the important.

Do only those things central to your job performance and likely to be noticed by top management and don't get hung up on perfection or develop tunnel vision; see the wider perspective. We looked at this in the *'Let's get it just right'* block in Chapter 4.

6. Use your initiative.

Ask to learn new skills, take on new assignments etc. This behaviour will show three things about you:

1. That you are well motivated.
2. That you are willing to take some risks by learning new things.
3. That you are willing to accept responsibilities.

Don't look constantly to other people for help and reassurance or to make decisions for you. You need to be looking for ways to demonstrate that you are competent and ambitious.

Here are some things you could do:

Try taking on some of your manager's tasks. Show that you are keen to improve your abilities and would regard any delegation from your manager as a new challenge. In most cases, it is important to be seen to back your boss as he or she may be the first person to be consulted if you apply for a promotion. So be your manager's right-hand person. Let them see they can depend on you and that it's easy to delegate some tasks to you because you do them so well.

Ask for extra responsibility. If you feel that you can handle a particular task you are not doing at the moment then put yourself forward for it. Now, if you do this, you may have to shed some of the work that you currently do in order to fulfil the new task effectively. You can't do everything – and it helps if you do have someone you can pass your work on to – maybe someone more junior to yourself, maybe a temp, maybe a student or someone else to allow you to take on the extra responsibility that you really need.

Volunteer for new projects. If you are not considered for additional responsibility, maybe it is because people don't know you want it, so step forward sometimes. Show that you're keen to have a go. Volunteer for some things.

Look for gaps. Take advantage of any opportunity to use and exploit your skills. These gaps might appear in your department or even in other departments. When people are ill or on holiday, look for ways of showing that you can handle certain aspects of their jobs too. You can even take on tasks that others refuse. Decide if it might be advantageous to take it on yourself if someone else refuses to take one on. Your boss may have a particular idea for improvement, but no time to work on the idea. That may be your big change. It's also a chance to create some new ideas. Look for new ways of tackling what may be routine tasks. Keep in mind that your solution should be practical and be seen as a high-priority by management. And when it succeeds, let others know about it and, of course, take the credit.

Take some risks. People don't grow if they don't take risks. For some women, the fear of failure is greater than the desire for success. To succeed, you have to put your initiative to the fore and not be frightened of what that might bring – whether it is success or failure.

Doing any of things are demonstrations of you using your initiative.

7. Let people know.

Stop waiting for people to notice you. If those who could help don't know what your ambitions are, then you may miss out on all the best opportunities. This is something that women might find difficult because we often wait to be noticed, especially when we are doing a good job. But being good at your job doesn't guarantee you are going to get promoted. It actually doesn't guarantee that you are even going to be noticed. You have to let people know that you are ambitious and you want to get ahead. Convince the powers that be that you have the qualities and skills necessary to achieve the promotion you want and equally, that you want feedback on what you do.

Ask your manager for a regular appraisal. Not only does this give you the opportunity to discuss areas for improvement, but it also emphasises your strengths to your manager. It's true that some male managers fear being totally honest with women staff just in case the women are going to completely collapse in pieces if negative comments are made. But you really need that feedback. Research seems to show that men get all the feedback that they need to improve; women get told what they are doing well and not as much about what they are not doing so well. You need to know what you are not doing so well so you can improve and show your manager that you have improved and you have stepped up your game.

Ask yourself these questions:

- *Who are the people with the power to recommend promotions?*
- *Do they know what I want?*
- *How can I demonstrate my ambition?*

The vigour with which you promote yourself within the organisation is going to be even more crucial to your success if you happen to work in an organisation that is unaccustomed, or worse, reluctant to promote women – especially into management positions.

8. Be visible and be prepared to stand out.

Women might find this a bit more difficult because we're not used to necessarily putting ourselves forward and standing out, but it is part of being visible at work, visible to your manager and your manager's colleagues about what your potential is. So get to know the people who matter. Let them know who you are, what you are doing and where you want to go. Becoming visible in this way is an essential part of getting the credit due to you and increasing your number of career options.

There are a number of things you can do to get yourself into the limelight. Some of these are altering your personal style and image. Your body language is well worth looking at here. In your workplace, look at the men's body language and the women's body language. It seems, for instance, that men stand and move far more confidently. They have an easier swagger. They are very expansive. They sit and spread out in the chairs that they sit in. They take up a lot of space. Now look at how the women in your organisation stand and move and see if it's true that when they stand they seem to be a bit closed in and their shoulders are round or they are holding something in front of them or crossing their arms. Their heads are down. Even their feet might be turned in. Now, if this is the case, it is giving a very submissive image of you to whoever you are talking to or being seen by – even before you open your mouth.

I am not suggesting that you have to start flinging your arms about and sitting down and spreading your legs in a chair at all, but I am saying stand up straight. It may seem really basic, but you would be amazed at the non-verbal messages given off by somebody's body language. So stand straight and tall, look at someone directly and clearly. And of course, when you do open your mouth you will have no problem about communicating very clearly and very directly.

And finally, look the part. What do I mean by this? I mean look the part for your next job. I am not one of these people who is prescriptive about what women should and shouldn't wear and whether they should wear makeup or not. That's not what I'm about at all. But look at the norms in your organisation and see if the people at the level above you dress differently – whatever that might look like.

You have to decide. But if you want your manager to visualise you at the next level they have to see you fitting in at the next level. Now, you may consciously choose not to do that. Well, that's fine as long as you are making a conscious choice, but it's worthwhile looking is there any difference between how you present yourself and how the people at the next level present themselves.

Here are some other things you can do to stand out:

- Organise social events
- Speak up at meetings
- Chair meetings
- Tell people your name and function if meeting them for the first time – whether that's inside or outside the organisation
- Get the credit for things you have done well
- Find out the best place to be seen and get yourself there and network

This networking thing is very interesting. People have said to me that women are not very good at networking. You know, women are excellent at networking. When we move house, within days we know the best school for our children. Sometimes we even move house for the best school for our children. We know the best supermarket. We know the best dry cleaner's. We know the best coffee shop. We know where the best childcare facilities are. We do not have a problem in networking to find out information. But inside organisations, we might have more of a problem in networking. I think that is because a lot of women feel less confident about networking when they perceive that the reason they are networking is to see if someone is going to be useful to them, because that is how they maybe have seen men networking.

Women tend to focus on building relationships, not just at how that person might be useful for them. I think we have to see networking differently. Networking is about building relationships. We also have to see networking as a way of making ourselves visible in the organisation. It's not about how you can use people. It's about how you can put yourself forward and make yourself available. So see networking in terms of "you give what you've got and you'll get what you need". This actually is the first principle of networking. And make sure that people do know who you are. Think of other ways you can increase your visibility at work.

9. Find a sponsor.

Find someone of a higher rank than yourself, who is important in the organisation, to assist and advise you in your bid for promotion and who will speak up for you. Mentors in the organisation are great as they can show you the way through all the roads, and byways and pitfalls in the organisational structure. Sponsors are even more important: someone who will be in your corner. Let this person know what your ambitions and achievements are and ask for their support.

Self-Reflection 3

Select which of these nine actions you are going to commit to as a priority and identify your first three tasks for each.

Five key actions to remember about yourself

So having looked at actions you can take regarding your career, here are some actions you can take related to how you view yourself.

1. Assert yourself.

- Be enthusiastic
- Behave as if you want and expect to achieve success
- Have the confidence to act in the way you think you should
- Pay no attention to how others react to you: that's their business, not yours

2. Believe in yourself.

- Establish a personal attitude that there isn't any problem, situation or task that you can't handle: because if you haven't got the knowledge, skills or information to do it now, you have the personal resources to find out how to do it later
- Be your own best supporter
- Only you can build the life you want!

3. Like yourself.

Instead of concentrating on getting other people to like you, like yourself. If other people's opinions are so important to you, you should definitely like yourself – how can you expect others to like you if you don't like yourself?

4. Look after yourself.

- Make yourself the most important priority in your life
- Look after every part of you: body, mind, emotions and spirit. See all these parts of yourself like rooms in a house that have to be aired every day
- Check at the end of each day that you have fed each part of yourself

5. Enjoy yourself.

If you don't then what is the point of it all? Build enjoyment into your day, your week and your life.

Chapter 9

Becoming the Leader You Are Meant To Be

This is the final chapter in your OPAL journey. We've looked at your leadership journey in your organisation and at how you can be at your best and perform at your best. We're now going to look beyond the organisation you are currently in and expand the focus to look at your leadership potential in relation to the wider community and society. You are the leader of your own life whether or not you move into a senior leadership role at work and you need to be able to access your best self wherever you are and whatever you do. Having looked at balance related to work and life, we're going to raise the focus of balance to include balancing who you are with who you want to be; balancing who you are with how you live and balancing the head and the heart as you **live** your leadership journey.

What is an inspirational leader?

First of all, here's a summary about being an inspirational leader, which you can use as a checklist as you monitor your own progress to leadership.

Someone who gives and receives respect

A person who both listens and is listened to: who values others regardless of status, age or any other differences.

Someone with clarity of vision

A person who takes substantial time out to plan and can communicate specific success criteria both in their work and personal life.

Someone who is motivational

A person who understands others and encourages individuals towards their goals with a wide variety of positive strategies.

Someone who is good to be around

A person who handles stressful situations well, does not judge, has fun and a high level of energy.

Someone who demonstrates flexibility and creativity

A person who is able to generate a number of solutions and can adapt to change readily.

Someone of integrity for whom honesty and trust are paramount

A person who thinks before speaking and can be relied on to keep confidentiality, tell the truth and follow through on commitments.

Someone who is prepared to show up, take responsibility and get things done

A person with a high level of confidence that's communicated verbally and non-verbally, who does not blame or encourage a blame culture and takes action appropriately and is not too proud to clean the loos when necessary.

Someone who stays abreast of the latest developments in relevant sectors of business and industry and is knowledgeable, experienced and open to learning

A person who takes obvious enjoyment working in a company they respect and support. Loves learning and speaks enthusiastically about the people and the job.

Notice that the title is about being an **inspirational** leader but if you look at the characteristics they are about the kind of person you are **being.** If you are authentic and working with integrity then people will want to follow you. They will be inspired as much by the person they see showing up as by any particular actions you might take.

Self-Reflection 1

How do you think you are doing on this scale? Choose one or two areas to focus on and two or three actions in each area to start working on.

So now let's take a closer and deeper look at you.

The importance of finding and revealing your Divine Feminine

I wonder how that phrase, the Divine Feminine, strikes you? Does it make you groan and think, 'Oh no – not that stuff'? Or do you feel a sense of excitement at the idea of connecting with a part of yourself that is maybe unexplored as yet? You might be thinking that we looked at feminine strengths way back in Chapter 2, so what's the difference between feminine strengths and the Divine Feminine?

Well, let's start with the physical. We are programmed by our sex and our gender to produce, to give birth. Whether or not we choose to give birth to children, we carry the nurturing skills in our genes to assist growth and provide love and care to new growth. So it was easy for us to develop the feminine skills of listening, empowerment and co-operation, which some men have to learn. But even if we choose not to produce children we can certainly birth new ideas, new ways of being together, new ways of being in organisations and give birth to the empowering of others. The Divine Feminine takes us *beyond* the feminine.

The emergence of the Divine Feminine is a journey so we can create a new world; draw new lines instead of keeping within the old lines. The focus is outwards but the expansion is from within: we expand our consciousness, which is expressed in new forms in the external world. Our liberation has moved on from the laws and constraints that hold women back to the liberation of the Divine Feminine in ourselves: the emphasis is on one's holistic wellbeing. The consciousness-raising of groups of women almost 60 years ago has become consciousness-raising for each of us as individuals, our own spiritual awakening. But not just for ourselves, for the communities we serve too.

We have already explored the need for feminine strengths in organisations. And we know that men need these skills too. In fact men and women both need a balance of feminine and masculine traits. But listening, collaborating, peace-making, being noble and good aren't enough to create the changes that are needed. If we are to call society to account for its humanity and to ensure our organisations don't exploit their suppliers and customers, and if we are to stand up for equality and justice at all levels, we have to get into positions of power and be comfortable wielding power.

The Divine Feminine is a powerful presence: unafraid, risk-taking, and fiercely creative.

Look at the examples of Boudica, Joan of Arc, Athena, Kali the Hindu Goddess of Destruction, the Suffragettes. Do we care enough about our world, our communities, our organisations to wield power, assert our values, engage in conflict and do whatever is necessary without getting intoxicated by power as we have seen men do?

The Divine Feminine is the connection to the consciousness of the feminine wisdom of the ages. It takes us beyond the sense of self and carving out our own destiny (we had to do that first; we are still doing that) but now we have to rise up with our Divine Feminine Power as a creative force and construct new ways of being. You don't acquire personal power or the Divine Feminine in you – you already have it – it's waiting to be released and revealed. Believe in yourself. Take five minutes a day to tune into that power in yourself and allow the Divine Feminine to surface in your heart so it can be expressed in the world.

So was the Dalai Lama right when he said that the world will be saved by Western women?

Western women have made more progress regarding their independence, being treated respectfully, having more rights and having legislation on their side. In many respects we are standing side by side with our male counterparts so we are best placed for the next push – and it will take a push because we have become complacent.

Some women don't think there is a problem and that the equality fight has been won. It hasn't. We'll know we've got equality when there are women at the top doing a mediocre job! Of course we don't want anyone doing a mediocre job but the truth is that there are many men at the top who are at best mediocre. Any woman at the top is outstanding. She has to be outstanding or she wouldn't have got there.

Other women have learned to fit the system so well they can't even remember what the fight was about. Can you swim with the sharks without becoming one? Some women can't.

And there are those women who don't even want to be considered as women, they just want to be seen as people. I don't think we can deny our feminine power or strengths, any more than we can deny our female bodies. We don't have to deny anything: we have to work to our strengths and remember who we are at our powerful core.

What is needed now is new ways of being powerful in the world.

So what has this to do with the corporate woman? With you?

Firstly, the corporate world employs millions of people and the number of working women is on track to be higher than the number of working men in the UK and in the US. There are a lot of people who work in businesses large and small – that's a lot of people to lead and a lot of leaders needed.

Yes, women have progressed, but we are still grossly underrepresented at the top. The Divine Feminine is about feminine **power** and this power is needed not only so that women can progress but so that they can change the systems. So far it's like women have been breaking into a prison and now they are trapped inside. It's going to take a lot more than feminine strengths to break out of the prison. It's going to take feminine power. That's what I mean by the Divine Feminine.

We are looking for the key to who we are as women in the world and in the world of work, which have been denied us in the past through patriarchy. We have become polarised men and women – our differences have separated us – men have the power but women may well be more emotionally intelligent. In organisations, the masculine culture often prevails. How can we find ourselves here? Yet we must for it **has** to change and it is women who will do it.

The key to who we are is inside ourselves: in our authenticity, in the acknowledgement of our feminine strengths and the use of the power inherent in the Divine Feminine. When the Divine Feminine rises in women their energy is magnetic and the sense of possibility endless. So I believe it is vital for women committed to their leadership journey to find the Divine Feminine in themselves and reveal it to the world.

Self-Reflection 2

Pause and think about the Divine Feminine in you. Can you feel it? Are you excited or nervous about accessing and releasing your Divine Feminine? Do you accept a responsibility that is much wider than your organisation – for your community? Women everywhere? The world?

In order to find our Divine Feminine we have to be clear in ourselves what exactly we think we are here to do in the world. We were put on this earth for a purpose and we need to be committed to finding what it is and fearless as we live it. We have to think bigger than our current job and we have to work from our heart. So let's look at how we begin to tap into our heart and find our best work.

Doing your best work – from your heart

There are four parts to working from the heart:

1. Identify the gifts you want to use.
2. Incorporate meaning in your work.
3. Set your parameters.
4. Contribute to an effective work community.

1. Identify the gifts you want to use.

Joseph John Campbell was an American mythologist, writer, and lecturer, best known for his work in comparative mythology and comparative religion. His work covers many aspects of the human experience. Here is one of his much quoted lines:

> *This, I believe, is the greatest Western truth: that each of us is a completely unique creature and that, if we are ever to give any gift to the world, it will have to come out of our own experience and fulfilment of our own potentialities, not someone else's.*

So how to look at your gifts? A gift could be:

- An activity you enjoy, like dancing
- A personal characteristic, like being a great storyteller
- A personal experience, like coping with the death of a child
- A talent or skill, like being an Excel wizard
- An appreciation, like opera or modern art

We can be wide-ranging in our exploration of our gifts always remembering that our gifts are to be shared, and when we share them we are actively in a heart space.

So how can you identify and use your gifts?

Self-Reflection 3

What is your uniqueness?
What flower or car would you choose to be? Why did you choose this? Choose three words that sum up that flower or car's essence. How are these words good descriptors of you?

Discover your "bliss"
When were you really happy? What gifts were you using?

Applying your gifts
When do you use your gifts? How can you bring them into work?

Check your answers with friends. What would they have answered for you? How accurate do they think your comments about yourself are?

When I first did this exercise many years ago I was taken back to when I was about 8 or 9 years old and the kids in our back street used to put on a show for the neighbours. We would bring out chairs and charge people one penny to see the show, which we performed on fruit boxes with cloths thrown over for a stage. My party piece was singing *Lipstick on Your Collar* by Connie Francis.

I loved the excitement and nervousness and then performing for people and people enjoying it. In my job now I do a lot of presenting at conferences and seminars and I get the same kind of buzz and satisfaction. So there seems to be for me a clear connection between what made me happy then and what makes me happy now.

I've done this exercise with many women and asked them to see if their heart sings, like it did when they were young. One woman told me that she loved to read and she loved horses. She lived on a farm and she used to go to the stable with her book and climb into the hayloft and read for hours. I asked her about her life now. Did she read? No she didn't have time. Did she spend time with horses or other animals? No she was always inside a building or a car. Did she have time on her own? Never. Most of us experienced happiness when we were children. We have to find it again. And once we have identified our gifts, what then? That's what the third question is about, applying your gifts.

Remember that your gifts could be an activity, a personal characteristic, a personal experience, a talent or an appreciation.

Some years ago I was invited in to an organisation to help them to set up a women's network. At the opening (there were about 80 women there) I asked them all to share something about themselves that they would like to offer to the group. In fact I was asking them about their gifts. One woman said that her child had died a number of years before and she had now set up a support group for bereaved parents and she wanted to let other women in her workplace know in case they knew of anyone who might be in need of such support.

Someone who loves meditation could offer to run a meditation group at lunchtime. An Excel wizard could offer to do a lunchtime problem-solving clinic. The woman who liked to read? She could organise a book club. The point is that this isn't just about doing something extra; this is about connecting with our gifts and sharing them. Using our gifts energises us and benefits everyone. We have to start seeing work not as a huge chunk of time that takes us away from our families and stops us doing what we want, but as an opportunity to use our gifts, to remember the happiness they gave us once and to recreate those conditions even inside the working day. This isn't more work; this is finding ways to do more of what you love!

2. Incorporate meaning in your work.

The next part of working from the heart is to look at how to incorporate meaning in your work. Sources of meaning can be:

- Vision
- Experience
- Calling
- Community

As a pastoral theologian, Brita Gill-Austern has a passion for teaching and creating a community of learning where the care of persons is embodied in a pedagogy that engages head and heart. Here is what she says about meaning:

Genuine meaning is never abstract; it is always personal. It is what moves us, stirs us and leaves us transformed... We live first; we reflect later. First, people need to articulate their own experience, then, to discern the unique pattern and unity that give their life meaning.

Self-Reflection 4

Picture your vision
What would our world look like if it worked right? Which parts of your vision do you care about passionately?

Analyse your experience
Consider all the aspects of your life: family, education, faith and philosophy, work, social context. List several influential life experiences, some turning points, some stand out moments that you want to explore for insights into what holds meaning for you now. Identify the patterns and the messages that came to you from these experiences that you want to carry forward.

Explore your sense of calling
Do you have a calling? And is it a whisper or a yell? Has your calling come from a strong gift waiting to be used; a particular profession specially suited to your gifts; circumstances that compel your response; an empowering vision?

Assess the meaning in your communities
What communities do you belong to and what meaning do they have for you?

Collect your ideals
Look at the previous questions in this part and then summarise the meaning you wish to express through your work.

Let's look at these self-reflection points in more detail. The first point about vision is a big one.

Based in Chile, Dr Alberto Villoldo's Light Body School training combines ancient shamanic wisdom teachings with cutting-edge practices in nutrition, biology and neuroscience to give you the tools you'll need to transform yourself, and launch a successful career doing what you love. Here is what he said about vision:

The nature of the cosmos is such that whatever vision you have about yourself and the world will become reality. As soon as you awaken to the power you have, you begin to flex the muscles of your courage. Then you can dream bravely: letting go of your limiting beliefs and pushing past your fears. You can start to come up with a truly original dream that germinates in your soul and bears fruit in your life.

What a powerful quote that is!

You may indeed have a vision, a passion, a big idea. It may be about setting up something in the local community, it may be about making the world a better place, it may be about changing a system in your organisation, it may be about getting to be on the Board so you can make big changes. A vision is something that is deeply important to you – something you are prepared to commit some time to.

I am an Interfaith Minister and I conduct sacred ceremonies for weddings, funerals and baby blessings. In Ireland some years ago we were not allowed to perform the legal part of the marriage so people would go to the Registry Office and do the legal part the day or week before, then have an Interfaith Minister like myself do a spiritual ceremony later, which would be the one they would invite people to. On behalf of the group of us in Ireland I applied for us to be accepted onto the list of solemnisers. We were refused. I appealed. We were advised to apply again. I did, and we were refused again. I appealed again and the appeal was refused. I appealed about *that* and finally – after three years – we were accepted onto the list so we can now do legal weddings as well as spiritual ceremonies. It was a long and tortuous process but it was the vision that kept me going: the vision of people being joined together in a sacred ceremony without having to sign up to a religious dogma to do it. A vision where a Hindu could marry a Christian and *both* traditions would be honoured in the same ceremony. That has given my work great meaning.

Now maybe you don't have a burning vision, but we have all had a lifetime of experiences. This is the second phase part of looking at meaning. It's very important to analyse key experiences or turning points in your life. Let me give you some of my examples.

When I was a little girl I wanted to be a priest. Of course I couldn't be but the sense of injustice and unfairness I felt when my brothers were serving on the altar and I couldn't even step onto it never left me. When I set up my business 30 years ago it was in the area of Equality and my work now always encompasses helping women to fulfil their potential and take their rightful place in their organisations, communities and societies. And I *did* eventually become a priest (although not a Catholic one!) when I was 50 years of age. So witnessing girls and women not being allowed their rightful place started when I was very young, and the pattern I kept seeing led me into taking action professionally, by setting up my equality business, and personally, by becoming an Interfaith Minister.

Another turning point was when I worked in a women's refuge for two years. I had been a teacher before that and was used to organising – and telling pupils what to do. But in the refuge, and being part of the support group of other women I learned about facilitating growth, not telling people what to do. I learned about holding a space for people so they felt accepted and loved. I learned about the difference between facilitation and training. And I learned to see the strength in every woman I met. These things were critical as I moved from teaching to consultancy, from training to facilitation and from working with children to working with women.

I could identify many turning points: when I became President of the Students Union at university, when I set up my business, when my marriage broke up, when I was ordained. By charting out all these significant events I could see patterns, I could see lessons that I learned and how I carried them forward. When we've had busy and full lives (hello, every woman!) it's too easy to get swept up by our life and feel that we didn't have much control over it. This question will help you to look at the choices you did make and the difference they made to your life. And by looking at the patterns in your life you can see more clearly which ones you might want to drop now and which ones you want to continue.

The third question is about exploring the sense of calling. Some people know from early childhood what they want to do. Some have a calling but see it as a pipe dream, an impossible wish. Don't rule anything out. If you have something that keeps nagging at you pay it due attention. It's never too late to fulfil a dream or answer a calling.

The fourth question to consider is about the meaning in your communities. We are all members of a number of sub-cultures: mothers, squash players, knitters, voluntary workers, church goers. Think of yours, both past and present. What communities do you belong to and what meaning do they have for you?

Finally, the fifth part of the exercise is to collect your ideals. Look at the previous questions in this part and then summarise the meaning you wish to express through your work. Working through this exercise alone could take some time so do actually give yourself the time to do it. It's your leadership journey, it's your job, it's your life.

3. Set Your Parameters.

The third part to working from the heart is to set your parameters. The parameters we set for ourselves determine the choices we make. It's important to be clear about what's important to you. Everyone has certain factors which limit their career plans, either limitations imposed on themselves or those imposed by external forces. The word "limit" is not necessarily negative. It can be very positive because it's taking a realistic look at who you are and where you want to be, so you can be happy with the choices you make.

There are three areas to look at.

1. Personal ethics

Your ethics set the boundaries as to how far you are prepared to go to get what you want and they are very personal to you. They answer the question: 'Does the end justify the means?'

2. Work values

Work values are the standards you hold in high regard in relation to the job you want to do. Values begin to develop in childhood and continue to develop through life. As with ethics, work values are a very personal thing and you will probably be happiest and most fulfilled in a job incorporating your key work values.

3. Personal boundaries

Boundaries are personal factors that set a limit as to how far you can go when planning your career. Your boundaries may alter at various points in your life, depending on your own circumstances, so they will need regular review to see what has changed.

Complete the following exercise to help you to establish your own boundaries and set your parameters.

Self-Reflection 5

Personal ethics

What are your most important personal ethics? The following phrases are often associated with ethics. Tick the ones that apply to you and add any of your own.

Acting openly with people
Being loyal
Having equality of opportunity
Working hard
Having a sense of duty
Upholding personal morality
Using power for the majority good
Being religious or spiritual
Maintaining a high level of commitment
Never willingly hurting anyone
Always acting in a forgiving way
Being honest
Being successful
Helping others less fortunate
Holding a position of status
Treating people fairly
Holding high family values
Winning at all costs

Work values

What are your most important work values and why? The following phrases are associated with work values. Tick those that apply to you and add any of your own.

Having authority over others
Being part of a team
Co-operating to get things done
Facing challenges
Influencing others
Learning new skills
Making decisions
Using creativity
Working in a tight structure
Gaining advancement
Being allowed to work alone
Being competitive

Coping with changes
Feeling secure
Leading a team
Making money
Taking risks
Working flexibly
Achieving excellence
Handling a variety of tasks

Personal boundaries

The following checklists will help you to establish your own boundaries.

Experience and education

- Are you experienced enough for the next job you want?
- Will you need additional training?
- Will your organisation provide such training?
- Will you need to improve your educational level e.g. obtain a degree
- Would you move to a lower grade, or sideways, to change career track and gain relevant experience?

Place of work

- Is there a particular region/country you prefer?
- Do you want to work in the city, town or country?
- How far are you prepared to travel to get to work each day?
- Do you mind travelling in the job?
- Would you be willing/able to relocate?
- If relocating, what type of house, school, area do you want?

Employment package

- How much more do you want to earn?
- What are you willing to sacrifice to earn more?
- Are you willing to take a reduction to get a foot in the door?
- Are you willing to earn the same for a while, knowing the potential for growth is there?
- Are benefits as, or more, important than salary?
- What benefits are important to you (e.g. flexible working, career breaks)?

Time factors

- Are you willing to give up leisure time?
- Do you want more free time?
- Would you work weekends?
- Are you prepared to bring work home at night and at weekends?

- Are you prepared to take less holiday?
- Are you prepared to do more travelling?

Non-work interests

- Are you willing to give up time spent with the family?
- Would you be prepared to spend less time on hobbies?
- Would you be prepared to visit your family less frequently?
- Would you be prepared to spend more money on childcare?
- Do you mind reducing your circle of friends?
- Are you prepared to adopt a new social life with new colleagues?

Now use these checklists to help you determine what your personal boundaries are and fill in the following form. Review these parameters regularly and particularly when going for a promotion or a change of career.

PERSONAL BOUNDARIES
Experience and education
Place of work

Employment package

Time factors

Non-work interests

4. Contribute to an effective work community.

The final part to working from the heart is to contribute to an effective work community.

> *'We hunger for community in the workplace and are a great deal more productive when we find it. To feed this hunger... is to harness energy and productivity beyond imagining.'* Marvin R Weisbord

Is your workplace working from the heart? If you are reading this book, you are likely to be a leader of a team, so however large or small your team is look at the questions below and see how many ways *you* can provide for your team to work from their hearts too.

Gifts

Are people encouraged to use creativity in designing the work? Are they involved in decision-making? Are results rewarded? Is quality performance emphasised? Are people given room to challenge the status quo and offer alternatives?

Meaning

Does your organisation have a clear vision? And is there a clear link between the dream and the action? Does the mission capture people's hearts? Is there a connection or a conflict between the organisational mission and people's individual missions? Does the organisation contribute to the wellbeing of society?

Parameters

Does the organisation give attention to people's practical concerns?

Vocational dreams

Are people in the organisation continually learning? Does the organisation encourage people to take responsibility for their own training and development, and provide resources for them to do so?

People

How much personal support do people get? How much teamwork and self-management goes on? How open is the communication up and down as well as across?

Nourishment

What does the organisation provide to nourish the bodies, minds and spirits of its employees?

Self-Reflection 6

How does your organisation measure up? What is important to you? What would you like to change? What obstacles do you expect to meet and how will you overcome them? What steps will you take to initiate change?

Nourishing yourself as you become an inspirational leader

So finally, let's look at nourishment, the final part of this chapter and the book. We're going to look at seven ways to keep things in perspective and seven ways to nourish yourself.

Seven ways to keep things in perspective

1. Have an immediate vision.

We talked earlier about whether you might have what I call a grand vision for how you want to make a difference in the world. But it's also important to have a more immediate vision: what do you want to be doing in three years, or in five years? What kind of life do you want to be living? Where? Who with? What work are you doing? I think it's always a good idea to think in 3-year cycles. Yes, you can change it if your circumstances suddenly change and your vision for the next three years might just be to keep doing what you are doing (because you're in a new job, because you have a new baby, because you've just relocated). That's fine too. But then *choose* that vision, choose that life, otherwise you'll feel that your life is living you and it will be easy to get despondent when the going gets tough.

2. Seek opportunities and take risks.

Whatever your vision, whatever your life, always be on the look out for an opportunity to do *more* of your vision. To get you from here, where you are now, to *there*, where you want to be in three years' time. Plan your own progression. Women are much more likely to wait and 'see what they have in mind for me' as opposed to going for what they want.

3. Don't aim for perfection.

This is a reminder about something we covered in Chapter 2 – don't aim for perfection. I'm repeating it here because it's so important. Not everything worth doing is worth doing well: some things just need to get done. If your standards are perfection you will constantly be feeling like a failure because you're not meeting them; it will make it harder to delegate and harder to admit your mistakes. This block has many knock on effects. It's easier to get rid of it.

4. Identify your service to the world.

This brings us back to what we looked at earlier in this chapter – what are you on this earth to do? What's your bigger purpose? It has nothing to do with your job. I read about a hospital cleaner who used to change the pictures on the walls in the wards where there were people in comas. He was asked why he did this when the patients couldn't see them. He said that his job was to assist the doctors in healing and *his* role in this was to provide the nicest possible environment for when the patients *did* regain consciousness. He didn't see himself as a hospital cleaner at all. And I heard of a hairdresser who described himself as a self-esteem consultant because when women left his salon they felt better about themselves, not only because he made them look beautiful but because he provided a listening ear to them. So if you had to describe your purpose in three words what would you say? Mine would be something like "Bringing Clarity to Confusion" because I realised that whatever area I am working in that is what I am doing. My service to the world is the clarity I can bring. But I ponder about this regularly and I invite you to do the same.

5. See the wider perspective.

This is different from seeing a grander vision. Seeing the wider perspective means that we don't get hung up on our own importance. Yes, we want to do a great job for the organisation we are working in, but we have to ask ourselves, will this organisation even be in existence in 25 years? Will anyone care in another two years what I am working on for 24/7 now? A project we have devoted the last six months to is suddenly shelved – it happens. We have to be able to bounce back from that. Yes, we need to do our best work, but we can't be too attached to the importance of it or to the results. That's out of our hands.

6. Form a relationship with your gene (genius).

There is a wonderful TED talk by Elizabeth Gilbert (who wrote *Eat, Pray, Love*). She talks about the importance of *having* a genius as opposed to *being* a genius, and letting this creative genius be expressed **through** you. It's a very interesting idea. She says that we all have one. It's like a separate self, sometimes it engages with us and we produce something amazing. At other times it seems to stand in the corner and ignores us while we slog away. It helps to underscore that fact that we *all* have a genius: we are all capable of amazing things and we should never forget that. I love the way she speaks and tells her story; I encourage you to watch her talk.

7. Balance who you are with who you want to be.

Working your way through OPAL should have certainly helped you to clarify both of these. Be specific about who you want to be, about *how* you want to be and plan your own programme on how to get there. If you want to be a great presenter and feel that right now you're not so great then watch great presenters and see what they do. Is it the way they stand, smile, make eye contact, use humour, tell stories? Detail the specifics, then you have a list to work to. *Now* you can make a plan on how to improve in all those areas. It's like your 3-year plan for your life – but this time for yourself. How do you want to be different than you are now? If you can't be specific about this not only can you not plan your development but you'll never know when you've got there!

Finally, what about the seven ways to nourish yourself? I'm sure you know these already, so let this be a summary.

Seven ways to nourish yourself

1. Be present in nature.

It's your best energy source. It's why so many leadership programmes include an element of the outdoors whether it's a walk, yoga on the beach, or white water rafting. I'm not a great fan of outward-bound courses myself but I am a great believer in allowing the energy of the land and the sea to seep into us, to encompass us, and affect every part of us.

Speaking of every part of us, the second point is about feeding all those parts: body, mind, spirit and emotions.

2. Feed all parts of yourself every day.

We need to see all these parts like rooms in a house, where we need to open the windows every day and let some air in. Check in with yourself at the end of each day about what you did that day to air each of those rooms. Five minutes here and there would do it, as long as you do *something*.

3. Laugh!

We've all heard the saying laughter is the best medicine, and of course it's true. People can even do classes now in Laughter Yoga. Laughter affects us physically – it reduces blood pressure, reduces certain stress hormones and can improve alertness, creativity and memory. So it's important to laugh hard every day – not just giggle. I live alone, by choice, and regularly laugh out loud on my own at something I read or see. Comedy programmes are favourites of mine. It's not only relaxing to sit down and laugh at a TV programme – it's good for your health as well.

4. Develop your creative side.

Write a poem, paint a picture, keep a journal, compose a song. This is a way to balance our right and left side of the brain. I first learnt this when I was studying English and Mathematics for my degree. I could spend hours solving mathematical problems then turn to write an essay about Shakespeare's Cleopatra and feel fresh. I learned to move easily between these two sides of the brain and found that it helped to keep me in balance. So if you spend a lot of time using your left side of the brain then you need to deliberately cultivate some right brain activity to keep yourself in balance and harmony.

5. Don't allow others to drain your energy.

We all know of people who come to talk to us about their problems and when they leave us they say, 'I feel so much better for talking to you.' And you? You feel so much worse because they have taken your energy. The **best** way to get energy is from source – the trees, the sea, nature – but the **quickest** way to get it is from another person who has more energy than us. So if you realise that someone is about to take your energy then think to yourself, 'I see you need energy but you're not taking mine' and imagine energy coming in through the top of your head and coming out through your hands to them. They *will* get the energy they need, but it won't deplete you. In fact, you will be energised too because you have opened yourself up to energy coming in to you from source. This really does work. I invite you to try it.

6. Take five minutes a day to relish THIS.

I started to do this 30 years ago when my brother, who was 29 at the time, was killed in a car accident. He was on the motorway early on a Sunday morning. There was only him involved. He was going too fast and the car turned over and he was killed outright.

When someone dies who is close to you – as I'm sure many of you know – it brings you face-to-face with your own mortality. It made me think – even as I was coping with his death – I'm on that motorway all day long. I'm up and down that motorway. That could be me. It could be any of us. You get up one morning, you go to work, and the next thing – you're gone. You are out of this life. Then I realised how often during the day and the week I would be saying things like:

Oh, it will be Friday soon and I can't wait.
I can't wait until it's 6pm and I can just put my feet up.
We're going on holiday soon. Thank goodness. I can't wait.

I was always not being able to wait for something in the future and it made me think, well, suppose there is no future? Suppose I never get to next weekend? Suppose I never get to 6pm tonight?

So every day I started to stop what I was doing and just for a few minutes, say to myself: 'I am really enjoying what I'm doing right now. I'm loving what I am doing right in this moment.' To look around me, to pay attention to what it is that I love and to keep myself focused on enjoying what I've got now. I'm not always focused on something in the future. I am living in the present.

7. Listen to your heart.

We've spoken already in this chapter about working from your heart, but we have to be able to open ourselves to *listen* to our hearts, so our best selves can guide us. I've found the best way to do this is by meditating – even 20 minutes a day will do it. Some people use a walk in nature; others take a bath. It's really about giving yourself some space and time to turn off your brain, to quieten your thoughts and allow inspiration to appear and for peace to settle inside you.

My final piece of advice for you is to never stop shining. Your only job is to be a magnificent woman – the rest will follow. It's not about having it all; it's about receiving it all, having a full appetite and living a full and passionate life.

I wish you a very fruitful career and a fun-filled and fulfilling life.

I will not die an unlived life
I will not live in fear of falling
Or of catching fire
I choose to inhabit my days
To allow my living to open me
Making me less afraid
More accessible
To loosen my heart
So that it becomes a wing, a torch, a promise
I choose to risk my significance.
To live so that which comes to me as seed
Goes to the next as blossom
And that which comes to me as blossom
Goes on as fruit.

by Dawna Markova

If you liked this book...

If you have enjoyed this book you might also like my book *Reclaim Your Power, Reclaim Your Life: Living Your Life as a Powerful Woman*. It's full of ways to help you to transform how you live your life – looking at all aspects of your life including both home and work.

I have also written a short companion guide to *Reclaim Your Power, Reclaim Your Life* called *Powerful Woman Tips: 100 Ways to Access and Live from Your Personal Power*, distilling some of the key points into Tips. You can dip into that book on a daily basis and use each Tip as your daily inspiration.

Testimonials

'Working for a large government department for many years, I have attended numerous training courses and heard many speakers, but absolutely no one has ever made an impact on me the way that Geraldine Bown has done and continues to do. My first experience of Geraldine's work was Jan 2006 when I saw her in a short training video on Positive Action for Women. Unlike any other training video, those few minutes made me sit up and listen! Geraldine opened up the whole question of what I could do if I wanted to and what my strengths as a woman were. The video left me wanting to know a whole lot more. I subsequently attended one of her training workshops. This course was pivotal in my life and gave me so many tools for me to be able to change my life where I wanted it to be. The result: I am now more confident, assertive, relaxed and happy, not only in my work but in my home life as well. All of this is directly attributable to Geraldine and her fantastic work. Anybody who is lucky enough to work with Geraldine or view her work cannot fail to be impressed. I personally endorse Geraldine Bown and her training products, I know they work, and they work well. I know they worked for me.'

Pam Dugdale, UK
Senior Manager, Government Department

'Geraldine Bown is one of those exceptional people who lights up a room as she walks in! Full of energy, fun and profound and practical wisdom. When I wanted a presenter and keynote speaker for my work, which led to the setting up of a Women's Network at Rolls-Royce plc, Geraldine was my first choice. Her knowledge and experience were invaluable, not to mention her dynamic and memorable style. I know that she is a real role model for women, full of integrity and authenticity, so that women who spend time with her feel inspired to take useful life changing choices. I wouldn't hesitate to recommend her as a superb teacher on issues to do with women in the workplace.'

Avril Carson, UK
www.avrilcarson.com

'Geraldine Bown inspired the development of The European Institute for Managing Diversity in 1986, of which she is a founding member and former Vice-President. Her profound knowledge and conviction of the critical importance of respecting and including the diverse cultural and demographic profiles of peoples, has been the guiding principle of the EIMD since its foundation. Today the EIMD is present in 30 countries throughout Europe promoting research, models and tools to help organisations leverage the differences of its persons – whether internal or external to the organisation. Geraldine is a marvellous communicator who transmits and inspires others in that in which she firmly believes: the rights of all to live and work in an inclusive environment. And particularly the empowerment of women who make up the community destined to make the highest contribution in the 21st century. Whether as a speaker, as a facilitator, as an author... Geraldine is and has been a guide for generations of men and women towards a new paradigm of management which embraces respect, emotion and spirituality, to address critical issues with a new dimension, in a changing socio-economic and political scenario, where values have evolved faster than the schemes and structures of institutions.'

Myrtha Casanova, Spain
Founder and Honorary President, European Institute for Managing Diversity
www.iegd.org

'I have known Geraldine for more than 20 years. One of her many qualities, which strikes me whenever I am with her, is her passion for women's development and the energy she consistently puts into it. Geraldine was working in women's development, Diversity and Inclusion long before they were "fashionable". The first time I ever heard the word Diversity it was in a conversation with her. Geraldine is very creative and I would say her greatest quality is her power to inspire. It was this quality I wanted to capture when I invited her to speak at the inaugural Extraordinary Women Conference and Awards, which I founded in 2008. She was one of the most popular speakers in April 2009 and as a result women who attended the conference later attended a 1-day workshop with Geraldine on Practical Spirituality. This too was amazing. Her perspectives on life are quite unique and I would strongly encourage any woman who is considering buying her books to go for it. She will inspire you to get in touch with a powerful inner "you", which you didn't even realise existed! Enjoy!'

Vicki Espin, UK
Director, Corporate & Executive Coaching Organisation and Founder of Extraordinary Women UK
www.cecoach.com

'I know Geraldine Bown as the most dynamic speaker both when talking to huge audience of hundreds of people as well as a workshop leader for smaller groups. She is teaching people to believe in themselves and gracefully and powerfully feel gratitude for who they are and for those around them. I met Geraldine back in 1997 and she spoke at W.I.N. for the first time in 1999. As both the participants and I loved her work, I have since invited her back to speak both in the plenary and run workshops on a number of occasions. She really listens to the women and she knows exactly how to teach and help them transform and be more of who they really are.'

Kristen Engvig, Norway
Founder and Leader of W.I.N. (Women's International Networking)
www.winconference.net

About the author

Geraldine M Bown is the founder and Managing Director of Domino Perspectives; a former President of the European Women's Management Development Network; a founder member of the European Institute for Managing Diversity; and co-founder of the Diamond Edge Programme for women leaders.

Geraldine has spent over 30 years working in the areas of women's development, diversity and spirituality. She is known for her transformational training and inspirational presentations. She is a past recipient of an ASTD Excellence in Practice citation for her Diversity work with PepsiCo in over 30 countries. Geraldine provides programmes and coaching for empowering women, and leadership programmes and one-on-one executive retreats for men and women in Connemara, Ireland.

She has co-authored three books for women managers translated into over 10 languages; co-authored From Diversity to Unity book and workbook with Mary Casey and authored two sets of Diversity & Inclusion Conversation Cards for leaders and managers.

Personally, Geraldine is a Reiki Master and in September 1998 was ordained as an Interfaith Minister and Spiritual Counsellor. She completed a Postgraduate Certificate in Spiritual Development and Facilitation at the University of Surrey Management School in 2007.

She is also a certified facilitator of SQ21 – the Spiritual Intelligence Assessment Tool. The assessment tool measures 21 skills that combine to create the ability to be wise and compassionate in our behaviours, while maintaining inner and outer peace – even under great stress.

Geraldine lives in the heart of Connemara, Galway in Ireland.

www.powerfulwoman.net
www.dominoperspectives.co.uk
www.interfaithministers.ie
geraldine@powerfulwoman.net

Printed in Great Britain
by Amazon